Tragedy
to
Triumph

by

Sharon Gregory

TM

Easy Break, First Time Publishing
Cupertino

ISBN: 1-891571-02-X

Cover design by: Entrusted Design, San Jose, CA

Printed in the United States of America

This book is dedicated to . . .

. . . the memory of my first-born son, Jeffrey Mark, so that those who knew him won't ever forget, and those who didn't will be able to meet him here and see how God used his life and death to change my life. . .

. . . the Lord Jesus Christ, without Whom I would be nothing.

Introduction

"How do you heal from the death of a child?" That question had been asked of me every time it became known that I had lost a child, so in 1991 I wrote what I have called "my story," a six-page document that was painful to write and emotional to read. The story was initially intended to be read only by my family, to show them how and why I have healed.

Almost no one in my family is comfortable talking to me about Jeff, either sharing good memories or the nightmare of his death. I believe that I am the only one who has ever gone through the entire grieving process. Perhaps as his mother the only way I could survive was to pursue it until I could accept it. But whatever my instincts were, I pushed through to the other side of grief and loss. It saddens me that I haven't been able to share the triumphant changes in me with my family. Although some of them read the original story, I have only had three responses to it and no apparent understanding of its main message—how God supernaturally changed me in the process.

Being healed doesn't mean that I don't still experience sadness, especially on his birthday, April 3, and on the anniversary of his death, November 15. I long to know what he would be like at the age of thirty. My memories of him are limited, and I must strain to remember the sound of his voice. But now I can see from God's perspective that there was purpose in his life and death, that God used my little boy to have a dynamic and lasting impact on me and on others through me.

I have called this "my story," but it is Jeff's story, too. In 1991, as I committed feelings and events to paper, it was vitally important that I create a lasting memorial of my son. I wanted people to remember him, to recognize the effect he had on the lives he touched, to actually see something positive from his death by focusing not on the tragedy but the triumph in my life—not just in spite of it, but because of it. This precious two-and-a-half-year-old left a powerful legacy, and his very proud mother is determined to share it.

Why a book? As people have read my story over the past few years, they have wanted to know more about how I got to the place where I am now and how I came to view every detail of Jeff's life and death from a perspective much larger than my own personal grief. Although the original version contained much detail of the way he died, I left huge gaps about my personal life and glossed over areas that I preferred not to reveal, only hinting at why I really felt so guilty when he died. I am now ready to bare my soul, revealing intimate, shameful things which I have kept hidden, events reminiscent of a soap opera script. I know I am not alone in having made wrong choices in my life, in having done things for which I have felt ashamed; I believe my transparency will help others understand that no matter how bad we have been, we are never too far away for God to forgive and change us. It is time to tell the entire story. (For obvious reasons I will apply fictitious names to some of the people I have included.) I will take you through the entire journey: my childhood experiences that shaped the personality, mind-set, and patterns which formed the bases for my choices; life with Jeff; Jeff's death; life after Jeff to the present day. This journey encompasses the agonizing grief, the anger, the desperate search for "why," the answers, the acceptance, the reconciliation with God, the forgiveness, the healing, the restoration.

As much as this is my story and Jeff's, it is God's story. Although a shock when it happened, my son's death was not a surprise. God prepared me for it, actually telling me it was going to happen. I believe this to be an incredible story, a dramatic testimony of God's power, mercy, healing, and His supernatural ability to give hope in the midst of absolute despair, creating a new life out of desolation, *"to comfort all who mourn. . . to give them beauty for ashes, the oil of joy for mourning, the garment of praise for the spirit of heaviness" (Isaiah 61:3).*

Whether a parent or not, everyone is touched on some level by children. I can imagine few things worse than the death of a child. Whether or not you have lost a child, know of someone who has, or have just had what seems to be insurmountable tragedies, you have probably blamed God, just as I did. I want you to see that everything has a purpose. *"To everything there is a season, a time for every purpose under heaven: a time to weep, and a time to laugh; a time to mourn, and a time to dance" (Ecclesiastes 3: 1, 4).* My desire as you read is that you would be filled with comfort, hope, a realization that GOD IS REAL. *"Blessed be the God and Father of our Lord Jesus Christ, the Father of mercies and God of all comfort, Who comforts us in all our tribulation, that we may be able to comfort those who are in any trouble, with the comfort with which we ourselves are comforted by God" (2 Corinthians 1:3-4).*

God sees it all, the beginning and the end. He knows every intimate detail about us, including our thoughts. He only gives us what we are able to handle, and there is always a way out—I'm living proof. After my husband and I met in 1990 and he learned about some things that I have been through in my life, he said I was "a walking miracle." He did not yet have a personal relationship with the Lord, but the triumph of my life was what first opened his eyes to a miracle-working God. I am a living, breathing, example of this verse: *"And we know that all things work together for good to those who love God and are called according to His purpose" (Romans 8:28).*

Although writing a book seemed an overwhelming task to me, I believe it was an assignment from God. For example, November 15, 1995, the 27th anniversary of Jeff's death, was a Wednesday and, therefore, our weekly Bible study. At that point I had worked up to the idea of expanding the original story to include more details, such as how I became a Christian, but I had much more to say and felt constrained by maintaining a short-story format. Because I had been recently reworking the story, the saddest memories were fresh in my mind, and I was very emotional that day and evening, even breaking down in tears when I shared with the group what November 15 meant to me. My friends wonderfully and lovingly comforted me and encouraged me in my writing, voicing that God, through me, was creating a work of substance that would change lives. Chuck Boone, the leader of our group, kept referring to my work as "your book," while I kept saying "my story." As we talked on, the idea of a book settled in my spirit and gave me such a sense of freedom. As the others continued talking, in my mind's eye I began to envision chapters in which every pertinent detail could be shared without limitation. But the most amazing thing—God's confirmation—came a few moments later.

To back-track a bit, when I wrote the story five years prior to that night, I never titled it. Although a very distinct title stuck in my mind, I felt it was too presumptuous of me to actually name it, never considering at the time to present it for publication. However, as I worked to expand the story, it occurred to me that it was now appropriate to name it, and that same title was all that I could think of. In five years I never told a soul what that title was.

Now, back to this evening I was describing. As we discussed my "book," Chuck dramatically stopped the conversation and said, "I know what you can call it: From Tragedy to Triumph!" That was the title I had held in my mind for five years that no living human knew about! I sat there with my mouth open, in total amazement, as did Chuck when I told him what he had said. What a confirmation! What an awesome experience and an assurance that I was facilitating God's will, that through the writing of these events His purpose will be accomplished and lives will be changed.

Preface
by
Amy Gregory

When Sharon, my stepmother, asked me to write an endorsement for her book, I was excited. The only other time I have felt so honored was when I was pregnant with my son. That was in 1990 before Sharon had married my dad. Because I was expecting a child, I was intrigued with how she had survived the death of her son. I remember asking many, many questions about her experiences. I wanted to know every detail about his life and death and everything she had gone through, to try to understand how she survived and became the strong person that I was getting to know. I felt so connected to her Jeffrey by then, that I decided to name my son "Jeffrey" as well, but only with Sharon's permission.

I will never forget the look on her face when I asked her if my son could have the same name as her son that had died. She started to cry and said she would be very honored.

After my own Jeffrey was born and he was old enough to understand, I began telling him about the uncle he was named after, whom he would only know through stories and photos. As he has grown, it is more evident to me just why I had to name him "Jeffrey." There is a distinct physical resemblance of the two boys, so much so that when my Jeffrey Cole first saw a picture of Jeffrey Mark, he thought it was a picture of himself. Amazing, since there is no blood tie between them.

I, along with the entire family, watched and encouraged Sharon during every stage of the writing of this book. Several of us read every section as soon as they came off the printer. We watched as she relived every part of the story as she wrote. And we watched the healing happen. As the book was completed, it was as if she finally closed a door on the past.

During the course of the writing, Sharon felt compelled to visit Jeff's grave. She hadn't been there for 26 years, but she knew that it was another necessary step in sorting all the pieces of the past. I went with her that day (you will read about it completely in the book) and remember it well. The cemetery looked different to her after all that time; although she knew what section he was buried in, we couldn't find his grave. After much frustration, we finally went to the office. When the clerk pulled out a file card with his name on it, it became all too real for me. . . and opened the wound again for Sharon. We both just stood there and cried. If my reaction was so strong, I could only imagine what her feelings were at that moment. This was *her* baby!

As others have read the manuscript, and as I have reread it several times, both the story and the effect it has on people amaze me. I am so proud of my stepmother—who is more like a real mother— for continuing on to finish this very difficult task. She has come so far and has taught me so much. Her life and story have given me hope and faith in my own life. I would say that Sharon knows me better than anyone else, so I know that God had a purpose in bringing us all together.

I believe this book is going to touch thousands of lives— male and female, young and old, those who have had children, and those who haven't. Many will be able to relate to the tragic beginning. . . and to find hope in the triumphant ending.

Foreword
by
Michele Webber

Just once in everyone's life there should be a Jeffy. There was in mine.

April 3, 1967, was the day of his birth. I was so excited rushing to the hospital, so anxious to see my sister's baby. And there he was, the only baby being held in the nursery, his reddish hair parted on the side and a profile that looked just like Mr. Magoo. I instantly fell in love.

I don't know how to put into words what this beautiful little boy meant to me or how to describe Jeff's extraordinary nature from the start. It would be easy to say that it was just the excitement of having a new baby in the family, but it was more than that. It was as though he had a special warmth, almost a magnetism that drew you to him. He was like a wise old soul in a baby's body. And when I held him, there was such a bond, such a joy, and so much love, I thought I would burst.

As the months passed into the first year, I found myself spending all of my spare time at my sister's house, playing with Jeffy and taking him with me everywhere I could—to the store, to the park, to see my friends. I would love to baby-sit even if Sharon wasn't going anywhere. One of my fondest memories involves a night I was baby-sitting at Sharon's and spending the night there. Jeffy and I had a great night of playing and reading and talking (as only Jeff could) until it was time to put him to bed—about two hours later than his bed time; I just couldn't resist being with him. My sister came home later and we talked until we went to sleep ourselves. It was in the early morning hours that Jeff started to fuss, and he called out for "Ann-eee." He was calling for *me*, for his auntie. That's how close we were. Sometimes I felt like he was my little boy. I often pretended that he was.

November 15, 1969, was the day of his death. I had been out Christmas shopping, only to come home to see the look on my mother's face. When she and my stepdad told me what happened, I stood in disbelief, knowing there had to be some terrible mistake; nothing would ever happen to my Jeffy. I looked down at the shopping bags in my hand that held the two new little outfits that I had just bought for him for Christmas. A part of my life died at that moment.

It's been 28 years and still there are times when I can't talk about Jeffy without crying. I try to remember the sweet moments, but instead I see the cemetery and a bunny rabbit headstone.

As my sister buried her son, I tried hard to bury my feelings. I felt it was easier to not talk about Jeff, not realizing how much my talking could have helped Sharon. I watched her trying to hold her life together, not knowing what to say to make it better. But that's how our family dealt with emotional issues—we just didn't talk about them. When we had to, it was never easy.

When Sharon told me she had written a book, I wasn't sure what to think. I guess, selfishly, my first thoughts were of sadness and of remembering, hurting, and crying. Then she asked me to read the rough draft. I cried a lot. But I was also able to laugh, to remember good things, and to realize what she has gone through in the healing process.

I am so proud of my sister and the person she is. I have always believed that if anyone was put on this earth to be a mom, it was my sister. From the time we were small, Sharon mothered anything and everything—her dolls, the neighborhood kids, and, especially, me. Even to this day, she has that same warm, nurturing, caring side that draws other people (including me) close to her.

I also want to thank my sister for asking me to be a part of this book. I am not a writer, and as I sit here struggling to piece together my thoughts and words, I want to thank her for allowing me to say what I have wanted to say for so long. I want to tell her how much I love her and always will. I want to tell her how I respect what she has done and how proud I am of her for having the courage to do it. But mostly I want to thank her for the greatest gift of all— letting me share in the very short life and the joy and love of a beautiful little boy.

1

The Fabric of My Life

I was two-and-a-half-years old when my sister, Michele, was born. It is, in fact, my first memory. I remember sitting in the back seat of a Forties-vintage green Plymouth, my grandmother next to me holding my brand new baby sister. I don't know how much I mothered my sister then, but I do know that by the age of four my innate maternal tendencies started blossoming with my dolls.

I can actually remember two of my dolls from that time: Donna, whose plastic skin turned dark brown and whose eyes rolled up in her head after I gave her a bath, and Howard, really a girl doll that had been my mother's as a child, the kind with the saw-dust-stuffed body and wooden arms and legs. Howard wore an old green and white dress. From that time on, I longed to be a mother, naming, dressing, scolding, feeding, teaching, loving, and making plans for many dolls and imaginary children. I lived in a world of imagination, which only became more vivid as I got older and went to movies and discovered a wealth of scenarios to relive in my mind.

The memories of my parents as a couple are all negative; their only communication I can recall is fighting. There were a lot of photos taken when my sister and I were small, the family posing together, smiling, looking "normal," but I do not remember any of those fun times. What is vivid in my memory is my mother being constantly angry with my father, my father drinking, and my father spanking me with wooden clothes hangers until they broke. Considering I was a well behaved child and only required a loud voice to be thoroughly intimidated, that was severe punishment. Since I was the older of the two, any offense was automatically my fault.

My father's drinking was a frequent issue for arguing. One of my worst memories, and probably why I was always afraid of drunk people as I grew up, occurred at a party my parents attended with us in tow. We often went with them to friends' homes and were just put to bed when we got tired. This particular night we had been put to bed, but I was not yet asleep because of all the party noise. Two voices—angry voices—came down the hall toward the room where we lay. When the door opened I saw and heard my parents yelling at each other. I do not know if they aimed for the room where we were or just tried to find a room where they could fight privately. My father was hitting my mother as he yelled.

This, obviously, was not a marriage made in heaven, and by the time I was six he had moved out; when I was seven, they were divorced. I remember asking my mother one night where he was, and she told me that he left us because he didn't love us. It was a devastating thing to hear; unfortunately, there were very few times during the rest of his life that he ever showed us that she was wrong. He only took us out once a year, usually to an annual picnic he attended, and spent much of the day correcting us and taking credit for raising us. I was very resentful of that, feeling that he was using us as trophies. My sister and I have discussed many times over the years our need to get approval from men, which we feel stems from the lack of a loving, accepting male parent.

Life with the three of us—mother, little sister, and me—was fine with me. At least my mother seemed happier, even though it was a struggle surviving financially on her own with two children. My father was assigned a fairly small sum for child support, but he wasn't very dependable about paying it, so my mother received virtually no assistance. She had to go to work, another adjustment for all of us, and was hired at Bank of America where she stayed until retirement. By this time, we had moved to a two-bedroom house in the Parkside District of San Francisco, the rent taking a large bite out of my mother's $300.00 per month. But she amazed us at how she made it all work. She made so many friends among the vendors along Taraval Street, many of whom were her customers at the bank, that we were afforded lots of "freebies": free entrance to the movie theater, free ice cream (no wonder I was chubby), free meat (Not steak again!) from the butcher in the grocery store because the butcher had a crush on her. So many people knew us and catered to us that, even though we had less than our friends who had normal families, we had places to go where we were special.

I look back at those years, when it was just the three of us, with happiness. She made everything fun. She made up special games to play and told great stories with voices she created that Michele and I still remember. She was athletic and could do things that we were never able to. We used to show her off to our friends by having her do hand stands, head stands, and cartwheels on our back lawn. She would even skate with us and play catch with us. No one else's mother could do things like that! She was also very pretty and young-looking for her age. Even when I was in high school and college, people thought she was my sister.

Michele and I loved her beyond words; she was everything in the world to us. We barely let her out of our sight, her friends dubbing us "the bookends." I remember when I was about ten years old and she had to have surgery, spending several days in the hospital. I thought I would die without her. Although we stayed with neighbors, I had access to our house during the day, so I would go there and smell her clothes and cry. Because she worked, she felt uncomfortable leaving us home alone all day during the summer, so she took us to the safe haven of our grandparents' home in Hollister for most of the three months. We eventually had a good time, but the first three days we two were miserable, mostly just crying and not wanting to talk to anyone. What a thrill for our grandparents! I'm certain they could hardly wait for us to get there every year.

I have been told many times that I am a very good mother, which I credit to having a very good mother. As I see it, the only problem with my mother is that she is a hard act to follow, being able to do so many things and do them well. I have never said this to her, but I often felt inferior to her, that I couldn't possibly be as accomplished as she at anything. She was beautiful and slender; I started out cute but turned into a plain, chubby child. She could play the piano; I couldn't carry a tune. She was good at any athletics; I have never been athletically inclined. She could dazzle us with her gymnastics; I couldn't get my chubby bottom off the ground. She had lots of friends; I had few as a child. My sister was no help either. She emerged as a beauty in her early teens, which left me as the less attractive of the two of us.

My admiration for my mother, coupled with my feeling inferior to her, resulted in a pattern of thought and action for my life. I could never allow myself to be put in a position where I was compared to anyone else, where there was a possibility of being second best. My best course of action was to be unique, in a class by myself, where there were no rules or guidelines but mine.

That was the beginning of several patterns which cemented the foundation of whatever Sharon was going to be. Probably the first, however, and the most pronounced was my sense of responsibility, not only in following through with tasks assigned to me, but my feeling that I carried the weight of keeping everything right in our world.

Because my mother had to work, I had to take care of my sister, making certain that she got home safely from school and generally watching out for her. I was also assigned household chores and responsible for starting dinner by the time I was nine. Since my maternal instincts were naturally strong, I gave the same attention to my mother's well-being, sort of becoming my mother's mother. I was extremely protective of her, often having dreams of her being in danger and me always there to rescue her. She had some friends of whom I did not approve, friends who smoked, used profanity, and went to bars, and I made my feelings very clear that my beautiful, innocent mother should not associate with them. I remember one night she had invited some people to our house who were a little drunk. What a thoughtful little ten-year-old I was, brewing coffee and practically forcing everyone to drink it. My mother was embarrassed and made it clear that my efforts were not appreciated. It was at times like this that I felt I was just in the way and that nobody really liked me, except for my mother, even though I had displeased and embarrassed her.

Since divorce wasn't prevalent in the '50s, I tried to hide the fact that my parents were no longer married. I lied easily, even to my best friend, saying that my father traveled on business. It became a little tricky when my mom dated and I had to explain the existence of strange men (and I did consider some of them very strange) in our home.

Although the shame of divorce did nothing to enhance my confidence and self-esteem, neither did my appearance. Throughout the elementary school years I was usually one of the tallest and heaviest children in my class. By the time I was ten, my waist was over 27 inches and I hit 110 pounds. I was teased unmercifully, especially from the children who lived on our block. In games I was always designated to be the bully, the witch, the monster, the teacher, the mother, whoever was supposed to be the biggest and meanest. I remember one "monster" game where we had built a fort in our next door neighbors' kitchen, using the table, chairs, and blankets. I, of course, was the bad guy/creature and had to chase the younger children, who crawled under the table and through the chairs. I valiantly pursued them, also diving under the table to crawl through a chair, hot on their trail. I misjudged the size of the space, however, and got stuck in the chair legs, dragging the chair with me. Everyone laughed. . . except me.

Another pattern that formed during those early years was my self-reliance. In my role as the "little mother" of the household, I learned to take care of myself. Since it didn't appear that others saw anything special in me, I tried to do some things with my own creative flair, at least pleasing myself. Until I eventually left home, my mother often complained that I was so "independent," that I just *had* to do things my own way. My strongest motivation all during school was that I did not want to be average or just adequate, I wanted to excel!

But the problem with self-reliance is that you stop needing others and start believing that your needs can be met only by your own efforts. Those parts of my life, including my real feelings and opinions, I kept hidden, shutting out most of the world, or at best keeping it at arm's length. If no one knew much about me, they could not possibly dislike me. My self-reliance was my protection, but in protecting myself from being rejected by others, I created an isolation that led to a pathetic loneliness. It is only in the past year that God has shown me how lonely I have been most of my life, and it has been with sorrowful weeping with my husband holding and comforting me, that I have mourned a lost childhood and have let healing come. I will discuss this in more detail later.

In my self-imposed isolation my imagination developed into an active fantasy life, where I was always beautiful, always the heroine, always sought after, and had a father who was proud of me. When we rode in our car after a movie, the car was transformed into a carriage and I was the beautiful, rich lady embroiled in some adventure that always ended well for me. When I played with my dolls, they would be the actors in elaborate dramas of my creation, the clothes and hair designed to fit each scene. My bike was my car in which I drove my eight imaginary children. They all had names and ages and I spoke out loud to them as I drove around our neighborhood, acting out my role as the quintessential mother. My sister and I spent many hours concocting plots for plays and imitating television shows, such as "Queen for a Day," made much more elegant by the clothes my mother let us dress in. In each game, I was smart, beautiful, and in control of the circumstances; I had the love and admiration of a gallant, handsome man; and I was never in the way.

I am embarrassed to admit this, but at least twice I can remember faking situations to get attention. The first occurred when I was in elementary school. My mother, her date, my sister, and I went to a park for the afternoon. My mother was engrossed in her friend and I felt left out; no one was paying any attention to me, so I wanted to make them sorry. I disappeared for what I thought was a long time, not returning to where they were until late in the afternoon. I was expecting a warm reception, wanting to hear that they had been very worried about me. No one even seemed to notice that I had been gone. Not a big deal, except to the child who desperately wants to be wanted.

Although longing for approval from them, I had an inherent distrust of men, except for the ones created in my fantasies. I especially hated my mother's dating and most of the men she dated. Aside from the fact that they were male, they were an intrusion into our close-knit, just-the-three-of-us world. When I was twelve, just about to enter junior high, my mother remarried, and my sister and I were devastated. In the first place, I felt that my step-father did not like me at all but preferred my sister; secondly, this meant that my mother did not need me anymore and I was just going to be in the way. Michele and I were doubly hurt that we were not told beforehand about their impending marriage. They eloped in August of 1957 while Michele and I were spending the summer at our grandparents', then notified us by post card. Although my mother's marriage made her happy and afforded us a much more comfortable lifestyle, neither Michele nor I ever got along well with our stepfather until each of us was grown and ready to leave home. His constantly negative attitudes and responses to us put my mother in the middle of many domestic battles. But aside from our disagreements with him, he was a good man and treated my mother like a queen, which was the only reason we weren't more rebellious.

I don't know when it began, since it always seemed a part of me, but sometime during my childhood I started "knowing" things. It was eerie as I started seeing scenes in my mind—different from my fairy-tale fantasies—that would eventually be played out in real life before my eyes. And every time the real-life scene would unfold, I would watch and hear it as if watching a movie, feeling a strange physical sensation that would remind me I had seen this before. I imagine I never told anyone about this because it was normal for me. I often had premonitions that eventually came to pass, and I can remember giving some warnings. I have always been extremely intuitive, sometimes just knowing something—or someone—without knowing why. My children learned to listen if I said I "had a feeling" about something, which made things easier if I said "no" to something they wanted to do that I felt was unsafe. Every time I have gone against my gut feelings, I have been sorry. This part of my makeup played a significant role in the precognition of my son's death.

My feelings about men became more positive in junior high when two of my teachers, Mr. Losada and Mr. Martin, took an interest in me, encouraging me in every part of my school life. Mr. Martin always made a point of complimenting me on my clothes, which was really a compliment to my mother, who sewed most of them through the seventh grade. Both teachers saw in me a bright student and pushed me to strive for the excellence of which they felt me capable. Other than winning spelling bees I had never been outstanding in any way in school. All of a sudden I stretched my academic wings and found that I was smart, that I could get A's, that I could function in advanced classes. It was a whole new world to me, the first time I had any confidence in myself. Those men worked at building my self-esteem. I will always be grateful to them, not only for the junior high years, but for later, as they took the time to follow my progress until I graduated from high school. Seeing their trustworthiness afforded me the option of allowing other males into my life. By the time I graduated from high school, I actually had more male than female friends, and after the age of fourteen almost always had a boyfriend. It was the same for Michele, as we both had a need for male approval and companionship.

I actually entered high school before I turned fourteen, having skipped the first half of the freshman year, joining my class in January, 1959. Although an accomplishment, it put me in an arena in which I was younger, less experienced, and less adequate socially. I had always been an "adult" child in many awkward ways, but only on my own turf. Although people who know me now would find it hard to believe, until my mid-twenties I was actually shy with anyone outside of my immediate circle of family and friends. My attempt to fit in with these high schoolers was scary.

It was during the high school years that I developed my chameleon personality. I wanted to be liked and to fit in so badly that I became whatever I thought people expected me to be. I would never dare confront anyone about anything, so I swallowed many disappointments. My attempts to control my mother's life and the behavior of her friends had met with unwelcome responses, so I decided to be likable, non-controversial, everybody's friend. I agreed with any opinion expressed and based my comments on what I thought other people expected to hear. It is apparent, upon looking back, that I did not have a personality of my own at all. I became fairly popular by the end of my freshman year, even elected class vice president. But my identity had no foundation.

My first steady boyfriend came along when I was a freshman. John was a sophomore, played the drums in the dance band, and was tremendously popular. I was flattered, but scared, that he had set his sights on me, especially since he was sixteen and I had just turned fourteen. We were worlds apart emotionally and experientially. He quickly came to realize how young I was but thought he was just the one to bring me into a rich, mature sexual experience. He concocted amazing schemes to afford us time alone, and I was too naive to catch on until he was attempting to remove my clothes. He came very close to rape one night when he showed up where I was baby-sitting, at which point I told him to get lost. He threatened to tell everyone that I had slept with him anyway, so I might as well give in. I didn't care what he did, I just wanted him to stay away from me. As it turned out, he pursued many girls who also rejected his advances, and, having eventually pushed too far, he was expelled from school. I went out with a couple of other boys after that, but I was never comfortable with them and never let a relationship develop. . . until I met Mike in my sophomore year.

Mike McDonell was a year ahead of me but attended another high school. His best friend, Bob, whom I knew, was our student body president and had invited Mike often to our after-school sporting events. I also enjoyed watching wrestling and basketball in the afternoons after school, and it was during one of those afternoons Mike noticed me and asked Bob about me. A group of friends planned a surprise birthday party for my fifteenth birthday and invited Mike to be the surprise guest. I had been told of him but did not actually meet him until the night of the party.

We met, liked each other, and started dating. At first all of our dates were double-dates with Bob and his girlfriend, Sue. We had a great time, but the best date was the first time we actually went out alone together. It gave us the opportunity to talk just to each other, to really get to know one another without the distraction or observation of other people. I knew then that I really liked him, and that was the beginning of a three-year relationship. I can say without any hesitation that he was my first love. We were considered the perfect couple, always having a great time doing wholesome things, including spending time with each of our families. For three summers I went with his family to their "camp," nestled in the woods north of

Fort Bragg. Aside from getting carsick each year on the drive in, I loved it there. We really believed we were in love and talked often about marriage and the future.

Mike's entrance into college while I was a senior in high school signaled the beginning of the end of our relationship. He was quickly assimilated into the college scene and had an immediate desire to date several coeds he had met. This really hurt me, since we had always had a great relationship and he had always made me feel loved and special. All of a sudden I felt as if I weren't good enough anymore. I was in my senior year of high school, was head pompom girl, a class officer, and very involved in the activities of my class. I wanted my last year to be full and exciting, and I wanted my boyfriend to participate with me as I had with him during his senior year. My high school events, however, were too immature for him now. So while he dated college women, I dated a few of the senior boys. Oh, the arguments! He was not happy that I was dating, and when he did come to our campus to watch me cheer, he expected that I would automatically give him my attention, that I would change any plans and leave with him. Most often after games a group of us would go out to eat. It just so happened that I dated a football player during football season and a basketball player during basketball, and as a cheerleader it was natural for me to hang out with all of them. Mike was not happy about that and made it clear. The two of us caused a scene more than once, with one of us stalking off in a huff. Sadly, our once excellent relationship deteriorated to the point of breakup as we realized that it had to be all or nothing; we could not handle sharing each other. Mike was not about to give up his college dating, so we had no choice. (As an aside, the friendship that Mike and I formed during those years has never been lost. Although we only communicate once a year, we have remained friends since we met in 1960.)

College overall for me was a dismal experience. My first disappointment was not being able to go away to school, that I had to stay at San Francisco State. Determined to make it a real college experience, however, I pledged a sorority, then watched my grades plummet to the worst in my life. I dated fairly often and even had four promising relationships that, for a brief time, I thought might become serious. One of the men talked about marriage and even pinned me (with his fraternity pin). The major factor, however, in determining the length of these relationships was sex. Each man had assumed that since I had had a steady boyfriend through three years of high school, that of course we had taken it to the inevitable conclusion. When it became clear that I was not going to accommodate their desires, they were gone.

Then, at one party, a sorority sister introduced me to Ted, who attended a community college in the area. We had a good time that night talking, laughing, and dancing, something we both did well. He had a good sense of humor and seemed comfortable with himself, both qualities I appreciated. We did not leave together, but he asked my friend for my phone number. He called that following week, the first of several phone conversations during which we got to know each other before he asked me out.

That first date began a relationship which included introductions to everyone he knew, including his family: mother, brother, aunts, uncles, cousins. I just seemed to blend in with everyone, and it was obvious that he was impressed and pleased by that, especially since he seemed to be getting more attached to me. And then came the moment of truth, which by then I was expecting and dreading. Would I sleep with him or not? Easy answer: NO. The difference this time was that he did not disappear. In fact, as we watched friends marry, he started talking about marriage. Of course, I had heard that talk before, so I had no intention of giving in to premarital sex. As I look back, I believe that we were caught up in the marriage mode of other young couples until marriage seemed like the thing to do. I cannot honestly say that we were in love.

12

So, we got engaged—ring and all—and planned a July 5, 1964, wedding. As the date came closer, we started fighting more and more until I actually called it off within the last month of countdown. Although my mother had made all the preparations and the invitations had been sent, she was glad that I changed my mind (he reminded her too much of my father). I should have listened to her wise counsel. He was terribly upset after his anger subsided and begged me to marry him. I can remember his taking me to dinner and then parking on a hill in San Francisco that overlooked the lights of the city on an amazingly fogless night. He then declared all the reasons why we should get married. What a wonderful life we would have! What an asset I would be to his budding career (as a department manager for a retail department store)! How would this look to people? His family loved me! Think of all the money we would have once he got promoted! And on and on and on. He even cried. I literally felt sorry for him so I tried very hard to see all the positive things that could come out of this union. I was a wimp back then, not confrontational, not aggressive, afraid that to be really myself (whoever that was) was to risk having people not like me. So, much to my mother's dismay after her warning that "he's just like your father," I gave in.

Walking down the aisle, my stepfather whispered to me it was still not too late to back out. For once, I wish I had listened to him. Where was the glow, the excitement that a bride should feel? I am fairly certain that I did not look very pretty either. Aside from my inner turmoil, the heavy headpiece flattened my hairdo, in my opinion, to the shape of a mushroom. Much worse than that, I couldn't shake the feeling that something was wrong. During the reception, Ted starting showing a more forceful side, dragging me around to meet everyone he thought was important (to him), telling me how to act, when to smile, how to cut the cake, actually talking under his breath to me through gritted teeth. He was very concerned about appearances and very impressed with anyone who had money or the luxuries wealth afforded; his main goal in life was to have a lot of money. By the time I had changed for our departure, I didn't even want to leave with him for the honeymoon. Aside from being nervous about our wedding night, I didn't like the attitude that was emerging.

But, off we went to Lake Tahoe to begin our blissful married life. For all his bragging about former romantic exploits, our wedding night was a disaster. Once we actually consummated our marriage a day or two later, to say I was disappointed with the entire process would be an understatement. I returned home completely baffled as to what the big deal was about sex. During those few days in Tahoe Ted's real personality revealed itself; he shifted from being nice to being critical of everything I said and did.

We arrived back at home before the end of that first week and stayed home only long enough to repack for a water-skiing weekend away with several couples, an invitation that he accepted without even asking me. I don't remember the location, but it was very hot and there was little shelter. Everyone was camping out (not my idea of a good time), but since we had no camping equipment we ended up sleeping in the car. Other than when we happened to run into each other, aside from being in the car at night, Ted totally ignored me. I was included in conversations only as an afterthought; if he wasn't impressed with my comment he said so. When I complained, trying to find out what was happening, he got angry and complained to everyone that I was the old "ball and chain." It was one of the worst times I had ever spent in my life and I wondered if this was what marriage was like. Sadly, it proved to be a glimpse of exactly the way our marriage would be.

As bad as that weekend was, the one following was even worse. Again, he accepted an invitation without consulting me, just informing me we were going. It was a weekend with a lot of people again (he really considered himself "Mr. Party"), all staying in a large cabin. I don't remember what we did during the daytime, but at night he totally ignored me, hanging out and drinking with the men, finally leaving with them to go to a bar. There was no discussion, he just told me and left. The women were all left behind and, unfortunately, I didn't know any of them. I ended up having to sleep (although for me it was a sleepless night) in a room with several of the women, the men staying out most of the night. I was very confused and upset, but he acted like this was normal and it was my duty not to complain. I was beginning to feel invisible. As bad as it seemed then, that was only the beginning.

Our home was a one-bedroom apartment on the corner of 48th Avenue and Judah Street in San Francisco, about two blocks from the beach. Living so close to the beach, we often heard the plaintive tones of the fog horns, which seemed a fitting sound track to the life we were living. I was working full-time at Pacific Bell, while he worked part-time at the retail store and attended college. I bore the largest responsibility for our finances so that he could finish college. We settled into a fairly uneventful routine in which he went to school during the day and worked at night until 9:30. Any free time we had was spent with his friends, either as couples or just him with the guys. There was never any discussion about it; he made all of the plans. Although I still was not a confrontational person, I let him know when I didn't agree or just didn't want to go out. Those conversations didn't go well; he always ended up really angry, generally swearing at me, and sometimes just walking out and leaving me alone. It got worse.

Shortly after we married, he stopped any physical contact with me at all. He would not have sex with me, would not kiss me at all, and as time went on he would yell at me if I walked around the house less than totally dressed. He wouldn't let me see him shave or shower. In four years of marriage I never once saw him do either; actually it was only a few times that I even saw him undressed. I questioned, pleaded, cried for him to show me some affection and to explain why he had no interest in me. He never had an answer, and if I pursued him for a response, he would pick up his pillow and a blanket and sleep on the couch. At first I felt there must be something very wrong with me. Here was another man that was supposed to love me who totally shunned me. Although Mike, my high school boyfriend, and I had experienced some intimacy, I was a virgin when Ted and I married. Was my lack of experience the problem? Since I had not been impressed with our honeymoon, it certainly couldn't have been that he was totally out of my league. I knew I was a sensual person and would have been a quick learner had I been encouraged or inspired. Now I was not only feeling invisible, but ugly, clumsy, unwanted, and generally a failure. But, it continued to get worse.

As distant and unkind as Ted was to me, he was charming, attentive, and affectionate to other women. He was especially attracted to my sister, which really made me angry, jealous, and hurt. At family dinners, he would sit with her on the sofa with his arm around her, totally ignoring me. She saw him as her charming, older brother-in-law who lavished her with attention, always wanting to invite her over and include her in things. At parties, he always had his arm around other women and would openly lavish compliments on them. Many times he would disappear with one or another for long periods of time. He continued to ignore me, while I wondered what they were doing but was too humiliated to call attention to it.

The second situation I faked to get attention happened while we were living in Marin County. I worked in San Francisco and took the bus across the Golden Gate Bridge to and from work every day. This particular week, my sister was staying with us because of a school vacation, and, because Ted was still in school as well, he also had time off. This fact caused me great stress since it meant that they were alone all day, lounging around in bathing suits at the pool. In the evenings, he doted on her and ignored or snapped at me, so one day I decided to make him pay. I regularly caught the commuter bus at the Ferry Building and maintained a consistent schedule—same bus each day, same time of day. One night I decided not to catch the bus, but to wait for the very latest one, wanting my husband to worry about me. I literally stood around in the cold just waiting, until finally the last bus made its run. I had no idea what I was going to say when I got home. My usual habit was to call him from the bus stop and have him pick me up, but I didn't even do that, so I would get home later and really look disheveled and upset. I walked all the way home, across a busy thoroughfare, down a hill, through hedges and bushes, and on an unpaved road. It was scary because I was totally alone and it was very dark. I was quite a sight when I finally walked in the door. What a terrible time I had had at the bus depot, I explained. A man followed me onto the bus and tried to molest me. I got off the bus to get away from him and caused quite a commotion, so the police were called. He got away, but they looked for him and kept me there to identify him, which of course wasn't necessary since he was not caught. They filled out a report and everything! (I told you I had a vivid imagination!) The police finally let me go to catch the last bus. I never gave an explanation as to why I walked home from the bus stop, and he never asked. And did all this drama hit its mark? Of course not; he didn't even seem to care. He was only annoyed that dinner was late.

Ted started criticizing me openly in public any time I opened my mouth, actually saying things such as, "Don't you ever think?" or "How can you be so stupid?" When we played cards or games with friends, he made fun of the moves I made and usually did not want to be my partner. It got so bad that our friends began to speak up, telling him to leave me alone and asking why he treated me that way. The only time he really showed me respect in public was when we went to company dinners where he tried to impress management with what a good guy he was and how happy we were. They all liked me, and he knew that he couldn't risk his normal behavior.

More and more people noticed what was happening and would reach out to me, mainly asking why I put up with it. As I said, I did complain and we had some real fights, but that just made things worse. When I reached the point of feeling like the world's most undesirable person, a new phenomenon occurred. Some of his best friends started reaching out to me in a most personal way, offering to "comfort" me, assuring me that I was extremely attractive and desirable. Three of them pursued me privately at parties, by phone, by suggestive comments, and compliments. I was amazed by the attention, even flattered, but I did not succumb to any of these advances. Although their intentions were not entirely honorable, their new interest in me gave me a chance to know them each as individuals, separate from their coupleness. I never spent any time alone with them, but their interest led to many interesting and fun conversations. They found me bright and knowledgeable, very quick on the come-back, and they enjoyed my sense of humor. Ted had tried to destroy all aspects of my personality, but this attention allowed me to blossom in spite of his oppression. Each of these men and their wives, as I became more open with them, commented in one way or another that they thought I was much smarter than Ted and that he was probably trying to diminish me to make himself appear larger.

One man who worked with Ted and had gotten to know him fairly well confronted me one night at a party with a probing question. Did I think Ted was a homosexual? He himself was "gay" (the term just starting to be used), so he said he recognized some tendencies.

The increasing stress took its toll on me physically; I began to hyperventilate often, which led to panic attacks. I developed multiple symptoms, the strangest being the rash under my wedding rings. It got so blistered and raw that I eventually had to take the rings off. As I felt sicker, I finally went to a doctor, who determined that I was healthy physically, just tormented emotionally. The rash on my ring finger, he said, was symbolic of the reaction to my marriage: an allergic reaction. Interestingly, he also asked me if I thought Ted might be a homosexual.

Even with all this stress, I still kept my problems to myself. The doctor knew, of course, my mother-in-law saw much of it, and I briefly talked with my own mother, but they were the only ones to whom I actually said anything. Again, I was alone, trying to take care of myself, hiding what I thought were my failures. Thank God, that changed one day in 1964. I was working at Pacific Bell then and was prone to having terrible monthly cramps. This one particular day, as I went to the "quiet" room to rest and wait for the medication to take hold, someone else was in the room with the same problem. Her name was Carole, and we worked in the same office. I don't know what opened the flood gates for either of us (she kept her problems to herself, too), but we poured our hearts out to each other. And as only God can arrange a divine appointment, it turned out that we were having exactly the same problems in our marriages. What a wonderful freedom for us both to finally talk to someone who could understand.

That day was the beginning of a lifelong "best" friendship that has taken us through many heartaches and celebrations over the years. It has sometimes been uncanny to us that we are so much alike and have been through many similar situations, but we know it's no coincidence that God matched us up. Carole is the friend I can always count on; she has always been there for me and has witnessed some incredibly life-changing events. Since that day in 1964, she has loved me, prayed for me, encouraged me, corrected me, taught me the things of God, cried with me when my heart was broken, rejoiced over my triumphs, and let me be transparent. Because she knows me so well, I know she understands and accepts how important she is to me. I wish that everyone could have a Carole in their lives.

When Ted and I were first married I started taking birth control pills; however, after the first two years of no sex, I decided to stop taking them, a decision that would have a profound effect on my life.

Sometime during 1966, a man for whom I had worked when I first quit college contacted me and asked me to work for him in a new venture: direct sales marketing of cosmetics. He had become a distributor and wanted someone who could learn all about the product and eventually teach his newly-recruited distributors. My personal makeup to that point was lipstick and mascara and my skin care was a bar of soap, so I was nervous about it. But the fact that I would be attending meetings at night would mean I wouldn't have to go home. It was also a chance to make some extra money. Ted and I had moved in with his mother in San Francisco by this time to save money for a little house in Pacifica we were buying. Any time we had a chance to get some extra money, Ted was all for it, so I didn't have any trouble getting started in this new sideline. Little did I know that my life was going to change dramatically.

Evening makeup classes began, and I was introduced to real skin care and makeup application. Ern Westmore, a Hollywood makeup artist, taught the classes, and I was impressed. I had always thought that since I had big eyes I did not need any eye makeup. I was delighted with the changes in my appearance as I learned the techniques. Co-workers at my day job were amazed by the transition, and with the enhancement of my physical features came a new kind of confidence. In contrast to the insults at home, I was now getting many compliments.

The room in which the classes were taught was large and filled with tables that had each been equipped as a makeup station. At one side of the room was a glassed-in office, where the company managers worked and observed us. Not too long into the training, I started noticing that one of the men in the office often stared at me. He actually sat back in his chair, arms folded over his chest, and blatantly stared. I did not know whether to be flattered or annoyed, but I was definitely self-conscious. Others began to notice and comment, telling me he was Bob Wyllie, the "boss." Rumor was that he was a flirt, so watch out! He never came out to talk to me, just kept staring.

For a public relations event, the company secured a booth at Brooks Hall in downtown San Francisco. The strategy was to do makeovers and distribute information in an attempt to recruit new distributors. As part of the draw, several girls would dress as Grecian goddesses (the product logo) and would circulate around the convention hall with the intent of drawing prospects to our booth. Much to my surprise, I was asked to be one of those goddesses. We were draped in gold lamé cloth, off one shoulder and tied at the waist. We wore gold sandals and Grecian-style headpieces. Since we were literally draped (and pinned together) each time, getting the right look was tricky. As we did the trial run the week before the convention, each one of us was dressed in costume and paraded before management. They wanted our makeup, of course, to be perfect, so they carefully assessed every detail.

Since I was still shy then and feeling a little out of my element in gold lamé, I hung back a bit and ended up being the last "goddess" through the management office. As I walked past the several men and started out the door, one of them said, "You're beautiful." Reflex action took over and I turned back to see who had spoken, then immediately around to see to whom he was referring. The speaker had been Bob Wyllie, and I was the only woman left in the room. I was shocked and embarrassed. I really couldn't believe that anyone would say that to me and mean it, but I was aware that quite a few people had noticed his staring and that the others in the room were watching us. I can't honestly remember if I said anything, but he got my attention. I noticed that he was handsome, with chiseled features, a cleft in his chin, a great smile, and a confident air. Although I sensed a red flag, I was flattered.

The convention opened up a whole new world for me; people were attracted to me, seemed to enjoy talking with me. I learned much about makeup and makeovers and how to sell, and

Bob Wyllie seemed to be pursuing me. I was certainly not used to such lavish attention. As Bob looked for occasions to talk with me, it didn't take him very long to notice my very low self-esteem. I recall his commenting that it was a crime what "that man" had done to me. He said I was like a person about an inch tall, and he was determined to correct a grievous injustice.

One night after we closed down, a group of us went out for food and drinks. Bob kept arranging for me to be near him as much as possible in the car and in the restaurant. He even asked me to dance, and I still remember the song: "Strangers in the Night" by Frank Sinatra. It seemed appropriate. It eventually became "our song." I was quite enthralled by this romantic behavior—but scared. I had not forgotten about his wife and two children, nor the fact that I was married. But, I let him drive me home and even let him kiss me before we got to my house. Trouble was imminent.

Once the convention was over, there were other nighttime meetings at which Bob and I saw each other, and each time he was attracted to me like a bear to honey. I determined not to be another notch on his belt, no matter how he affected me. My resolve was short-lived. One night at the Jack Tarr Hotel, he made his most aggressive move yet: he put a hotel room key in my hand, told me he had ordered a bottle of champagne, and would meet me there. After much wrestling with myself, and even going as far as getting my coat and starting to leave, I went against my better judgment and met him in that room. I felt like a character in a soap opera script—sleazy, but at last desirable. Also, by this time I had some personal feelings for this man. After that night, I realized what honeymoons were supposed to be like. Knowing Bob's reputation, I expected that I would never hear from him again, but I was wrong. This sordid beginning developed into a full-fledged love affair. Yes, we actually did fall in love and spent as much time together as possible, which was difficult since we both worked and had spouses. He had done it before and was good at it, but living a double life was a stretch for me.

Life at home for me was the same: dismal, unloving, uninteresting, with constant shunning or criticism. Our behavior was scrutinized by my mother-in-law, who loved me and could not figure out what was wrong with her son. Actually, he bossed her around too, but since she has always been an over-indulgent mother (she actually ironed his underwear!), she let him. So, confined the majority of the time to that oppressive environment, I thought about Bob.

One morning during that summer of 1966 I woke up feeling very tired and nauseous. I had to ride the bus from one end of San Francisco to the other (I lived by the beach and worked at the Ferry Building), and every day I fought what I thought was a touch of flu. But the nausea did not go away and I became suspicious that it was, in fact, morning sickness. Can you imagine the anxiety I felt as I contemplated pregnancy while being married to a man who wouldn't touch me? How does one explain this?

After a couple of months and a visit to the doctor, my worst fear was confirmed: I was pregnant, at least two and a half months along by then. As the doctor congratulated me, I wilted. What was I going to do? Ted was going to pick me up from there, and I was terrified to face him. He knew what kind of symptoms I had been having, so he must have been suspicious though he had never said anything. When I got into the car and he asked what was wrong, I just very quietly told him, "I'm pregnant." He never said anything as we drove home. Once we got home to face his mother, he told her the "good news." She looked shocked since she knew about our lack of intimacy, but she went along with it. Ted actually seemed pleased and said he couldn't wait to tell everyone. His bosses would love it! He made phone calls to spread the news! Eventually his mother asked me if we had ever actually had sex; I lied and said, once.

I was stunned by his reaction but went along with it as well, figuring that I had gotten away with it and everything was going to be fine. The only explanation I could suppose, since we never once discussed it, was that this baby would do much to enhance his image. What a lucky break for him; he got all the credit without having to be intimate with me. The fact that we were in the process of buying a first house was the perfect touch.

Of course I told Bob I was pregnant. He offered to arrange and pay for an abortion. I was appalled and hurt that he would suggest it. Even though I didn't know much about the subject, my maternal instincts were too strong to kill my baby. My main concern with him was to not break up his family. Since Ted had apparently taken ownership of this situation, I decided to make the best of it. We might have had a terrible marriage, but I would be the best mother I could be and do whatever was necessary to bring up my child in a real family. Although Bob called me constantly at work and asked to see me, I told him it was over, that he already had a family to take care of, and that I would not be a party to destroying it. I eventually stopped taking his calls, but it broke my heart. I really loved him and wished more than anything that we could be sharing this experience together.

2

A Child Is Born

Jeffrey Mark was born on April 3, 1967, at St. Francis
Hospital in San Francisco after thirty hours of labor. I was gloriously
happy. I felt fulfilled, complete; I was a mother. But looking at my son
caused me anxiety because I saw his father; he was a miniature
replica of Bob, down to the cleft in his chin. I could hardly wait to
get him home and begin our new life, but I was nervous about how I
would explain his unique, and unfamiliar, features to the family. I
was sad that his father was not sharing this time with me, that he
couldn't celebrate the birth of his son, that I had to live a lie. And I
still loved and missed him.

Although I was excited to be home with my baby, our
homecoming was not what I expected. As I was laying Jeff in his
bassinet for the first time, I heard a voice—inaudible, but very clear—
—saying, "He will not live past the age of two." A lightning bolt could
not have jolted me more. Since I have always had premonitions and
other insights into the future, I believed it and was terrified. But
believing it did not force me to accept it. I justified it by trying to
believe it was just my maternal concern about something terrible
happening to this beautiful child. Like every parent, I feared ever
losing him. I never told anyone about that voice of doom until after
Jeff was gone. Whenever it spoke a reminder, I stuffed it deep down

inside me, afraid that to ever tell anyone would make it come true. When he was still an infant and I was trying to explain to a newly-married couple how much I loved my son, I said, "I would gladly give my life for him." In retrospect, I know that was my way of fighting back, to tell whoever or whatever was planning evil for my child to take me instead. He was worth so much more and he needed a chance to live.

I threw myself into raising and enjoying this little boy, who became the center of my world. His hair was reddish at first and thick enough for me to give him his first hair cut at eighteen days old. The red soon turned to blond—almost platinum in the summer—and his eyes were a deep blue, just like his father's. No one seemed to seriously question his coloring and build, which were also like Bob's. This was strange since Ted was a short, dark-haired Italian. His mother was convinced that Jeff looked like Ted when he was a baby. He and I still had never discussed the conception of this child, both of us continuing to live a lie. But my son and I had a home, and Ted had the image of the all-American family man.

I had not talked to Bob since the middle months of my pregnancy, my way of shutting the door on that relationship to allow both of us to go on with our lives and keep our families intact. Little did I know that he was trying to keep track of me, even going through public birth records to see when our baby was born and the sex and name. I saw Bob every time I looked at my son, still missing and loving him, but I was determined to leave him alone.

When Jeff was just a few months old, I was hired by Jay, an independent distributor from the company where I met Bob, to do some part-time promotional work: teaching classes, giving makeup demonstrations for women's groups, doing the makeup for fashion amateur shows. Since Bob was still with the company, he did business with Jay from time-to-time and found out that I was working for him. They arranged a surprise for me, Jay suspecting that we had had a relationship but not knowing about Jeff. Coincidentally, one day when Jeff was eight months old, I was unable to get a baby-sitter so I took him with me to Jay's shop. Bob was there. The look on his face when he saw his son, a veritable clone of himself, spoke volumes. It was a heart-stopping experience for both of us.

We spent time together that afternoon in the back of Jay's shop, talking, getting reacquainted, adjusting to a shared parenthood, delighting in our son, and finally gushing out the love, the missing of each other, the yearning to be together. He told me that I had taken him completely by surprise; he had never expected to fall in love with me. And sitting between us was the product of an illicit, but loving, union. Now what were we going to do?

After that reunion, we could not stay out of each other's lives, talking often on the phone, trying to see each other whenever possible. Bob was enthralled by his son and wanted to see him often. Here we were again, sneaking around, living double lives. The more we saw each other, the more we wanted to be together.

My home life was deteriorating; Ted and I were barely speaking to each other and he was rarely home. Aside from my infidelity, which I assume he suspected, we had other serious issues that led to the demise of our relationship, one being his fixation with money. My spending money on anything that wasn't food was not allowed, and I always regretted it if I "disobeyed." I remember ordering some children's encyclopedias for my very bright child, and he was so infuriated that he not only didn't speak to me for several days, he also took away the check book, all the cash that I had, and the car keys. And he left early every day and got home very late. Before Jeff was born we had moved into our new home, a small house on a steep hill in Pacifica, a small, out-of-the-way town on the coast whose closest shopping was some miles from our house. I was literally a prisoner in my home with no money, no one close to help me, and very little food. I was angry and scared. Back then, I was still not assertive or confident in my own abilities and certainly unaware of any other resources of provision. On Sunday of that week, while

Ted was entranced by a sporting event on television, I packed Jeff's diaper bag, took money and the car keys which he had tried to hide, sneaked down the stairs to the garage, got into the car, and left, fast. I don't remember the rest of that day, except that we ended up at the home of friends in San Francisco who took us in and listened as I finally revealed the truth about our life. Most of it was not a surprise since they had seen firsthand his treatment of me ever since we had been married. What was a surprise for them was hearing the truth about Jeff. They were amazed that I had pulled it off. Once their shock wore off, they gave me their support. One of them was a lawyer, so I got my first legal advice as well.

Bob was worried and infuriated at the way I was being treated. He wanted to be with us and take care of us, so he made a very big decision—to leave his wife for me. I was scared, not only of how to extricate myself from my current life, but of playing the role of "the scarlet woman." I was now approaching 24, was not very worldly, and had very low self-esteem. The new course of events took on a life and speed of its own, totally out of my control.

Bob's sister, Jane, and her twin daughters, Susan and Sherie, lived in Reno, Nevada, so the plan was for Jeff and me to move there, establish the six weeks required residency, and obtain a quick Nevada divorce. First, however, we decided to make a short trip to Reno, find an apartment, get to know Jane and the girls, and find out how to proceed with my divorce. We planned to drive together to Reno. On the way, however, we had an appointment about which I was terrified. Bob felt he had to tell his parents about everything, that they had to meet me and be introduced to their grandson. He had always been his parents' pride and joy; they not only doted on him, spoiled him, bailed him out of problems, but followed him whenever he moved so they could be near him. So far they only had granddaughters, so he was certain the news of an almost-two-year-old grandson would be a cause for rejoicing. For myself, I felt like a hussy, an evil home wrecker, and I wanted to hide. I hated the role I was now playing, but I was drawn to the man I loved, so I followed his lead.

Bob arranged to meet his parents for dinner at a restaurant on the water in Berkeley, a favorite of theirs. They thought they were just meeting him on his way to Reno and were delighted by the invitation. Little did they know that their lives would be changed in a moment of time.

Tom and Lucile Wyllie were in the restaurant lobby when we arrived. Not one to beat around the bush, Bob immediately said, "Mom and Dad, I'd like you to meet your grandson." They were completely shocked, but for Grandma it was short-lived. She took one look at this miniature Bob and fell in love. And it was mutual as Jeff walked right over to her, put his little hand in hers, and proceeded into the dining room. Grandma looked as if she had been given the most precious gift, and her emotions were revealed through expressions of amazement, joy, and tender tears. That was March 25, 1969, a meaningful date for her: her mother's birthday. She could not take her eyes off that little boy. The discussion was bittersweet; along with this beautiful grandson came the realization that their beloved—and unsuspecting—family was about to be torn asunder. Papa's emotions were obviously ambivalent, as he wanted to envelope his son's son but held back because of what Jeff's appearance meant. It was a time of ecstasy and agony. And then there was me! Jeff was one thing—this other woman was quite another. They excluded me while listening to Bob, then grilled me and warned me, telling me about Bob's family and what this was going to mean. I understood all that, of course, and felt totally ashamed. In the end, however, I believe they knew that to not accept me was to be alienated from their son and grandson. I choose to think that they truly believed that I loved their son.

We arrived in Reno very late that night, having driven over snow-covered highways. Snow would be a new experience for Jeff and me, but he missed our entry into Nevada as he was fast asleep in the back seat. Jane, Bob's sister, greeted us as we parked. When we opened the door to the back seat and she saw the sleeping child, she said, "Oh my God, it's a little Bob!"

Our stay in Reno was productive but wreaked emotional havoc on Bob's unsuspecting relatives. Jeff, of course, just moved right into the hearts of his aunt and cousins. From that very first weekend there, you could count on seeing Jeff with a twin on each side. Before I left that first weekend, Jane and I became true friends, bound with a strong tie that still exists. As with my friend Carole, neither time nor distance changes the ease and closeness of our relationship. By the time we were ready to return briefly to California, I had begun my residency, had rented a furnished apartment that I would move into in a week or two, and had said good-bye to a new family that looked forward to our return. Now, of course, we had to tell everyone else. I couldn't believe this nightmare was happening to me. In all of my fantasizing and role-playing as a child, never once was I the "other woman." And I knew the worst was yet to come.

Finally, Ted and I had a conversation about whose child Jeff was—the only conversation we ever had about it. Strange, don't you think, that he never once talked about my being pregnant when he knew there was no way it was his child? What kind of man reacts like that? His objective in reacting to our leaving and our marriage ending was merely to make it clear that he would not give me any money at all. I eventually took a little of the furniture, which I had to sneak out while he was at work since he intended to keep it all, but I never received any compensation from the house. At the time, it didn't matter to me.

My family was shocked. My mother knew the kinds of problems we were having and saw how he treated me, but I was still the "bad" one; I had not been raised that way, what was she going to tell her friends, etc. My stepfather was very angry and voiced his feelings very strongly. It was ugly, but we all got through it.

Telling Bob's family was the worst, and he kindly excluded me from the initial conversation. He had Jeff and me tucked in at his parents' house, just a few blocks from what was soon to be his former home. The four of them, he with his wife and two daughters, aged fourteen and twelve, spent a sleepless night, crying, explaining, and pleading. My having to meet them the next day was the worst experience yet, as you can imagine. Linda, his younger daughter, was the only bright spot. She not only instantly adopted and loved her little brother, but accepted and loved me very quickly as well. While I was still living in Reno, Bob would occasionally fly up with her so she could spend the weekend with us. She was the most precious, loving child, and it was a delight to have her around. "Sissy" and Jeff became inseparable during those weekends and closer still after we moved to San Jose when my divorce was final. She and I spent a great deal of time together as she grew up, even traveling together, and we too have a special bond that has lasted these many years. As she grew up and encountered her own challenges, it was often uncanny how much alike we were.

Then, near the end of March, 1969, Jeff and I left for our stay in Reno. To be honest, I was relieved that we were able to live so far away from conflict for a few months. Surprisingly, we loved Reno and settled into a good life, free from disapproving family. I pretended that we were a normal family, that my "husband" traveled on business and was only able to get home on the weekends.

We had a wonderful time with Jane and the girls; we were all very close. Although I didn't go out socially, except on occasion with Jane and her friends, it was great having full-time baby-sitters/entertainers for my son. I remember one funny incident that reflected the girls' special care of Jeff. They were often indulgent with him, giving in to his every desire. One day they let him taste prune juice, and he liked it. They let him have his fill, then were very distraught when he had diaper "blow-outs" several times the next day as a result of all that stimulating juice. At one point Jane and I found the three of them in the bathroom, Jeff standing in the toilet, being rinsed off by two frustrated girls who had tired of the traditional diaper-change-and-wipe method. This was the biggest mess they'd ever seen, so in desperation they decided to take a new approach.

Once my divorce was final, Bob moved us to San Jose where we rented a three-bedroom house. His divorce was not yet final, as he had filed in California, but we moved in together, Bob and Jeff as much father and son as if we had always been together. Jeff became the center of attention for the entire family, especially for his grandma who thought the sun rose and set because of him. Papa quickly jumped in with both feet, too, and spent much time teaching him how to use tools and do other manly things, thoroughly enjoying this small man-child shadowing him.

As for Jeff, he was big for his age, broad-shouldered and sturdy, legs stocky, very strong and smart. To say he was "busy" is an understatement. How many eighteen-month-old children can dismantle their cribs by unscrewing the bolts and screws with their own little fingers? As he approached two, an incredible sense of humor emerged with an ability to recognize what was funny about someone and then mimic it in a way that made the person laugh. His humor also showed when we played "Hide and Seek" in the house. His consistent hiding place was under a cushion on the sofa. Of course, he was hardly noticeable with the big cushion lying on his little body—several inches above the other cushions—and his tennis-shoed-feet sticking out at one end. We would go through the house pretending not to notice him, saying, "Where's Jeffy? Where did he go? Where's Jeff?" From underneath the cushion would come a little voice: "I don't know!" He was so much fun!

Grandma remembers one night as she was knitting when Jeff picked up the skein of yarn and ran all the way across the room with it to tease her, while inadvertently unraveling her work. She laughed and enjoyed his antics as much as the rest of us did—even when she was on the receiving end of his mild destruction.

Even more pronounced than his sense of humor was his sensitivity to the moods and feelings of others, along with a mature capacity to reach out, to love, and, in his precious way, to comfort. I saw this demonstrated to adults as well as other children, and each time I was amazed and touched, wondering what special things were inside my child. I will try to describe it. Throughout the course of his "busyness," no matter where he was or what he was doing, he was somehow able to zero in on anyone who was troubled. He would stop what he was doing to go to that person, wrap his little arms around them, place his cheek lovingly against them, hold on quietly, protectively, soothingly, as if he were somehow "making it all better." This was something special, certainly not normal behavior for a two-year-old.

Jeff was enthusiastic about everything (except for the sound of large trucks and the claws on a stuffed koala bear that he owned) and always ready to go somewhere. Everywhere we went, he seemed to command attention, sort of becoming the mascot in places that we frequented, such as the barber shop. He jumped into everything with abandon, so anxious to do and know whatever was going on. Jeff was always the first one to jump off the diving board at Grandma and Papa's house, not caring if anyone was ready to catch him, yelling, "One, two, three, go, Geronimo, go!"

When around his Papa, as I have already pointed out, he was a virtual shadow, grabbing the lawn mower, edger, and other tools to do "what Papa did." I remember one time, when Papa wasn't watching him, Jeff was determined to figure out how to turn on the edger. We told him "no" and to not touch, but Papa scolded us, saying that children are told "no" too often, that they need to experience things, that they were his tools and he could let Jeff use them if he wanted. Well, while our backs were turned, Jeff did get the edger going, and that thing took off by itself—not on the edges of the lawn either! There went Papa, eating his words, chasing the edger around the lawn.

Another useful skill his Papa tried to teach him was fly-swatting. Like a proud and mighty warrior, he charged around the yard with his own fly swatter, swinging, whacking, and whooshing at every critter within striking distance. Even with all that enthusiasm, Jeff wasn't able to catch them, and after every attempt he would dramatically say, "Missed it!"

In his exuberance to explore he occasionally got hurt but hardly slowed down. When in the kitchen with me he often stood on a chair to watch what I was doing. One day when I was making toast for him, he climbed from the chair to the counter to look inside the toaster to see how it was making toast. He slipped and fell with his face against the toaster, leaving a horrible burn on his chin. He barely whimpered and soon forgot about his injury in the rush to go outside. His apparently high pain threshold was some small comfort to me after he died.

The ability to climb, of course, opened up new avenues of acquisition for Jeff, which was the source of a few headaches for his dad and me. For instance, very early one Saturday morning before we were awake, he climbed up and reached his bottle of Flintstone vitamins, which he loved; one a day was just not enough. This was in the days before child-proof caps, so I stored the bottle on the top shelf of a cupboard. Bottle in hand, he sat on the couch and watched Saturday morning cartoons as he ate Fred, Barney, Pebbles, and Dino. By the time we got up, he had the colors all over his lips, loose vitamins scattered around and between cushions, and an almost-empty bottle. Our pharmacist friend recommended a dose of mineral oil, so his enjoyment was short-lived.

Jeff's habits included ardent thumb sucking. In an effort to curtail this, we tried applying a hot, peppery liquid used to dissuade stubborn little thumb suckers. He, of course, hated it and decided to get rid of it. Climbing up onto the bathroom sink from the toilet, he opened the medicine cabinet, extracted the "bad hot stuff," opened the bottle, and poured it down the drain.

His greatest love, which also led to his tragic death, was cars and pretending to drive. For some months we had a friend, J.D., living with us who owned a classic 1956 Thunderbird that Jeff loved. J.D. often sat in it with him, letting him pretend to drive. But that was not enough for Jeff. One Saturday morning (again) while we were still asleep, he pulled a chair from the kitchen to the front door, climbed on it to unchain and unlock the door, let himself out of the house, closed the door behind him, and got into the unlocked T-Bird so he could "drive." It took a while for us to find him because of the closed front door, but when we did, he got a spanking.

Bob's most tender memory of his son, which he shared with me recently when I told him I was turning my story into a book, was Jeff's learning from him about the moon. Bob would often stand outside at night, Jeff usually on his shoulders, and they would look at the sky, seeing the stars and moon. Bob taught him "moon," and every time they would be out together, Jeff, with that innocent excitement of a child, would say, "Moon, Daddy, moon!" Bob could barely finish telling me without crying. It was such a simple thing, but one of those priceless moments between parent and child that lives forever in the heart. Bob was only with Jeff as a full-time father for the last nine months of his life, so those few lasting memories are precious.

The three of us settled into a new life together, Jeff stealing hearts and pulling the entire family together the way only a child can. We bought a house not far from the one we had rented and toured through it often as we watched the final stages of construction, Jeff, of course, inspecting every nook and cranny. We were excited about choosing carpeting and draperies and about our impending marriage, which was planned for January, when Bob's divorce would be final. That would begin 1970 for us—together, a real family, in a new home. I had been accepted and assimilated into the Wyllie family and, aside from my own family's resenting my new life, I was happy.

3

Tragedy

A month or so before Jeff died, things changed—he changed.

First, I began having nightmares about him being run over by a car in front of our house. Each time they were so real and so frightening that I awoke crying and went to his room to be sure he was there. I would just sit by him, watching and touching, listening to his breathing, willing that he would not be taken away from me. Afraid to give voice to the unimaginable, I never told anyone about the nightmares until after his death.

About two weeks before his death, Jeff's behavior changed dramatically. He would awaken from his afternoon nap hysterical. He seemed terrified, as if he had had a bad dream, and he clung to me for at least an hour, holding on for dear life. He wasn't able to articulate what it was, but he was clearly frightened. When he would finally release his hold on me, he would lie down on the couch with his dad for hours, not moving, content to be in the safety of those big, protective arms. As you can see from what I have described of his personality, these behaviors were not normal for him. I became more scared every day, afraid to think the unthinkable, still not voicing my fears to anyone. I tried looking for other explanations, like a passing sickness.

I suspect that somehow he knew he was going away. In the years that have passed since then, I have heard and read stories where young people, shortly before their deaths, knew or sensed they were going to die.

My son died on Saturday, November 15, 1969, Moratorium Day during the Vietnam War. How ironic that the one day soldiers stopped killing each other, Jeff had to die. Following are the day's details.

Jeff and I had a lot of errands to run that day while his dad worked in San Francisco. We were to meet him at Grandma and Papa's house at dinnertime. Jeff was always anxious to go out, so he was usually in a hurry to get himself dressed. That day, however, he refused to get dressed, cried that he did not want to go (which tore at my heart later), even hugged himself tightly so that I could not remove his pajamas. I told him where we were going, including to the barbershop for a haircut (which he normally loved doing), but he cried, "No!" I agonized later that I forced him to go, that if we had stayed home that day he would not have died.

We ran our errands, returning home with a back seat full of groceries, parking in the slightly inclined driveway. As I grabbed a couple of bags and reached for my son, he declined the offer of help with his usual independent response: "Jeffy do all by self!" As I headed for the front door, assuming he was following me, I heard the phone ringing, so I hurried inside to catch it. I stayed on only long enough to mentally jot down the phone number in San Francisco where Bob was working. I realized as I hung up that Jeff had not come into the house, so I went right back out the front door to retrieve him and more bags. The driveway was offset from the front door, so you had to go to the end of the front walk to see it. As I was walking toward the driveway, I heard a man yelling, "Help! Help!" When I saw the driveway, my heart stopped. My car was half-way in the driveway and half-way out into the street, and the man across the street was holding it from the back to keep it from rolling. Jeff was under the left side of the car, his feet toward the rear, the front left wheel on his head. I remember screaming his name. Reacting instinctively, I got into the car, started it, and moved it off of him since my neighbor could not move it forward and could barely hold it stationary. I pulled Jeff out and turned him over as people poured out of houses to see what had happened. Someone said they called the fire department and an ambulance. Their voices sounded as if they came from a distance, and I remember feeling like a spectator. I know I went into shock. I just sat in the street with him (I can still remember what I wore that day), trying to clean the blood out of his mouth so he wouldn't choke, saying over and over to myself, "So this is how it's going to happen." I put my hand on his chest and it seemed so flat and still. Was it crushed? At one point some well-meaning woman tried to pull me away, as if not watching him would make the horror less real. I viciously fought her off, like an animal protecting its young.

It seemed that the rescue team took forever, although I knew deep inside that it really didn't matter. My son was not alive. So strange, I thought, that he only had a small scrape on his face and a little blood from his mouth. Since the paramedics could not find any sign of life, I was not allowed in the back of the ambulance with him. I rode in front, listening to the machine pumping oxygen into his lungs, begging a God I did not know to let my baby live.

I never saw my son again. The doctor explained to me that he had died instantly from a fractured skull and probably never knew what happened. How can I possibly explain in normal words how I felt? How can I relate something so devastating as to be indescribable? Not only was I emotionally destroyed, I was in physical pain, as if I, too, had been run over by that car. I became sick to my stomach and spent what seemed an eternity of suspended animation in the emergency area bathroom. I locked myself in and vaguely remember the nurses knocking on the door, asking if I was all right. I don't remember whether or not I even answered them. I felt that half of my body had been blown away, and I was absolutely certain my life was over. The next thing I remember, I was injected with a heavy dose of medication which made me lethargic—it was a huge effort to move or even to talk—but it could not possibly dull such overwhelming grief. It was incomprehensible. It couldn't be true. I wanted to die.

A police officer came to interrogate me, and by the time I had finished the story, he too was in tears, sharing my pain. He talked about his own small children and how he couldn't imagine losing one of them. Bob was finally reached by phone, and I had to tell him that his son was dead. He had to drive the fifty miles from San Francisco knowing that. I will never forget the look on his face when he came into the room, a combination of devastation and utter disbelief. I don't remember our exact first words, but I know that he asked if I was all right. I can only imagine what I looked like by then. When we were able to, we pieced together, with the police officer, what probably had happened.

After I had started for the house with the groceries, Jeff got out of the back seat and into the front seat behind the steering wheel, which was witnessed by my neighbor who had tried to stop the car from rolling. The car was a 1966 Thunderbird, which had an emergency brake that automatically released when the car was put into gear. What we surmised was that he had shifted out of Park, the car started to roll, and either he got scared and tried to get out, or he fell out and the door slammed shut and knocked him under the front left wheel. I had left the door open, intending to take out the rest of the groceries, but when I got to the car that second time, the door was closed. It seems almost impossible that a child could be thrown in such a way as to land under the car far enough for the tire to roll over his head. But now my nightmares were reality; he had been run over by a car in front of our house.

4

Aftermath

It was by the grace of God I survived the next few days; I didn't think I would and I didn't care either way. After leaving the hospital that day we went to Grandma and Papa's, where I had to face everyone. In my drugged state, the faces that came and went the rest of the day were a blur as I sat in a recliner in the living room with a roomful of people staring at me. No one knew what to say or do with or for me. Bob never let down until we went to bed, then he cried all night as I held him. I could hear Papa crying in his room down the hall. So many people were devastated that it added even more layers of grief to my shattered spirit.

My words are not sufficient to describe the agony I went through in preparing to bury my baby. Having to choose a casket which would be his final bed was torture. That there were so many small ones to choose from made us painfully aware of how many children die. Because he was all boy, we chose a blue one. For his headstone we picked a plump, cartoon-type rabbit, his right ear flopping forward, a figure you would expect to see in a child's room. Then, which last name should we use on the headstone? He was really a Wyllie, but the majority of his short life was with Ted, who started out as his father and who had loved him. We decided to use both last names to give recognition to both dads. I had to select an outfit, but I knew I couldn't dress him in it. I picked an outfit that Grandma had just bought for him, brown corduroy pants and a matching shirt with stripes in several colors. Would he need shoes? I knew he would need his favorite blanket, since he always slept with it while sucking his thumb.

We decided on a short graveside service at Oak Hill Cemetery in San Jose. Although it was the middle of November, it was a sunny day. I was comfortably warm in my knit suit, not needing a coat that afternoon. There are big trees next to the area where he is buried, and I remember the sun filtering through the leaves and branches, each ray a tiny spotlight on the place where my son would rest. I don't remember any of the service itself, but I can still see in my mind that little blue casket on the ground in front of me. Unable to accept that I was burying my baby, I cried out over and over, "He's just a baby; he's just a baby!" My crying came from so deep inside of me that it sounded primal. It was almost unbearable, and as much as I desperately willed it at that moment, I did not die.

As we were preparing to leave the cemetery, the funeral director tried to tell me that Jeff hadn't been hurt badly, that he was a little angel up in heaven now. Not hurt badly? He was dead! I recognize that he was trying to give me comfort, letting me know that Jeff hadn't been mauled or endured a long, painful death, but I couldn't accept what he said. An angel? There was no God and there were no angels, and I resented his feeble attempt to placate me. Years later, after I became a Christian and knew the Bible, his comment about Jeff being an angel resurfaced in my mind. A verse in Hebrews talks about "entertaining angels unawares," and I couldn't help but wonder about my son's purpose here since so much had happened around and because of him.

The next days were torture as we tried adjusting to a life without Jeff. The tiniest of children fill up the biggest places in our lives. I strained to hear my child's voice, but there was no sound. The emptiness in the rooms reflected the emptiness in me. There were practical things that had to be attended to that made his absence even more heart-breaking. My wonderful family, directed by Jane, anticipated the needs and relieved me of many of those difficult tasks. The car that killed him was taken away so I never had to see or drive it again. His clothes, toys, and furniture were packed for me. We left that house forever, temporarily moving in with Grandma and Papa until our new house was finished. Jeff had been excited about moving to the new house. When we would go there to see how it was progressing, he would explore every corner and cupboard and hide in the closets, waiting for us to find him. Once we moved in, I kept expecting to open a closet and find him there.

After the first week, Bob decided we needed a diversion, so he talked me into seeing a movie. I don't know why—and it seems insane as I relive it and write about it—but after the movie we went to the house we three had happily shared such a short time ago. I remember it was dark and cold, but I don't know if the power had been turned off or if we chose to leave it dark. I can see in my mind's eye now going into Jeff's room, seeing his bed disassembled, his mattress up against the wall, and boxes of clothes and toys. It was more than I could bear. I broke down, turned to the wall, and started pounding my head against it.

Two weeks later was Thanksgiving, but to me the concept of being thankful was a travesty, and the day was a disaster. Bob spent most of that day trying to anesthetize himself with alcohol. He too was carrying a burden of guilt. The emergency brake on the car had been faulty, and he had intended to fix it but had never gotten around to it. In his drunken stupor late in the afternoon, he forced his way onto a friend's motorcycle and took off at high speed. I knew he was trying to hurt himself. When he didn't return for a long time, we sent people out to look for him. It was getting dark when I finally saw him riding in a golf cart, driven by a kind man who witnessed the accident, rescued him, and brought him home. As I remember, he had hit a curb and flown off the bike, either Bob or the bike hitting a fire hydrant. His eyebrow was hanging off his face, attached only by a few hairs and skin, and his leg was a mess. So again I was on my way to the hospital. The next day when I went to see him, I fainted in the hospital corridor. I was standing by his gurney while he was waiting to be X-rayed, and the next thing I knew I was in an X-ray room myself being revived with smelling salts. Bob had told the nurse what I had been through and she was very compassionate, allowing me time to just lay quietly for as long as I needed.

When Bob finally came home from the hospital, his eyebrow was reattached and his leg was fully casted. At last I had someone to care for again, but I also had to do all the driving. Since Jeff's death I had not driven at all; the thought of getting behind the wheel paralyzed me. I could hardly ride in a car. Now I was forced to drive, and I was both scared and sickened.

One night we planned to go to dinner at Henry's High Life in downtown San Jose, famous for great steak dinners. It was an easy drive straight down Monterey Road to Market Street, and the cool winter evening was clear. As I nervously followed the road where it veered onto Market, I saw flashing red lights in the middle of the street. As we got closer, I saw an ambulance and police cars, smashed vehicles, and a bloody body lying there. I panicked, and then, I guess, I blacked out. I kept driving, but I don't remember anything until I recognized Bob's voice yelling at me, his left hand grabbing me. My foot was still on the accelerator so the car was still moving, through red lights, across a very busy intersection congested with early-evening traffic, and veering toward the wrong side of the street with oncoming cars. My memory of the rest of that night is gone; I don't know if we ate and I haven't any idea how we got home.

Then there was writing thank you notes, which I had to handle as Bob threw himself back into his work once his leg was better and allowed for more mobility. Since he left early in the morning to drive to San Rafael, close to two hours away, and didn't return often until midnight, I hardly saw him. I was isolated from the world, and I was so lonely. Spending so much time alone with no one to talk to or take care of caused me to focus on everything negative, especially my guilt, which was almost as overwhelming as my sadness. I felt absolutely responsible for my son's death. I should not have taken him out that day; I should have listened to his pleas not to go. I should have been watching him every single moment, making sure that he had followed me into the house. At the core of my soul I felt I was a complete failure. I had been given this beautiful child to take care of, and I had let him die.

I truly believed I was being punished. I had had an affair, adulterous on both sides. I conceived a child, about whom I deceived everyone, I broke up a family, and I was living in sin. What better way to destroy me than to take away the most precious thing in my life? Although I bore the guilt for what I had done that resulted in my son's death, I also blamed God. He could have let Jeff live when I begged for his life. He turned a deaf ear to me, so I would never again attempt to talk to Him, would not acknowledge Him in any way. I became hostile to the world around me as well, feeling that I was owed something. As I isolated myself more, I began spending a part of each day at the cemetery sitting by Jeff's grave, talking to him. I missed him so much, I just could not let go. It broke my heart to be there, but I needed to feel close to him. I guess in a way I was burying myself as well.

I ached every time I saw a child. I recall one day when I again shopped at our regular market and was waiting in line. A mother with little children standing in front of me began yelling at one of them. To me, her tone and words were cruel, and I was horrified when she started hitting the child in the head. It took all the restraint I had not to shake her and tell her that tomorrow her children could be dead.

Those close to me soon learned not to mention anything about God. Scott, a Jewish friend of ours, seemed determined to change my mind, so he often brought up the subject. Each time he tried, he got a verbal explosion from me, so determined was I to make myself crystal clear.

The doorbell rang one afternoon, and I opened it to two smiling, booklet-toting Jehovah's Witnesses, eager to share their God with me. I let loose on them, asking them to explain why my child had died. They literally ran down the walk, never to return!

Bob realized that I needed to be pulled back into the world of the living. We started talking about having another baby, which I wanted more than anything. I soon had an agenda: to have another baby and to make some sense out of what happened, to know where my son was. Was there an afterlife? Was he there? Could he see me? Could he hear me talk to him as I sat by his grave? Did he miss me? I could not become reconciled to the picture of him lying in a box in the ground, so my search for answers began.

5

The Search

Bob and I were married in January, 1970, and then moved three times, finally settling in San Mateo. We were blessed with two more beautiful children: Shana Sharleen, born December 16, 1970, and Robert Michael, born June 7, 1972. They were the most darling, precious babies, and I, again, was in my element; I felt fulfilled. People have often asked me if I was afraid of having more children. What if I lost another one? I used to joke that I wanted to have a lot of babies—spares—in case I did lose another one. I can say absolutely that I never had the same fear with these two children, never a doubt about their safety, knew with a certainty that the same thing would not happen to them as with Jeff. I knew that as definitely as I knew that Jeff was going to die before the age of three. It wasn't anything I did to know that, it was just in me, I believe, from God.

My search for answers began in earnest when some people entered our lives who had information tailor-made for my investigation.

In the course of business dealings, we had occasion to meet many unusual (a euphemism for some of the element Bob attracted) people, one group of whom claimed to be psychics. Having had premonitions, prophetic dreams, and other foreknowledge most of my life, I was immediately drawn to them, desperate to get "inside" information, a higher level of revelation. In particular, I clung to Betty, who was the obvious leader of this group, asking numerous questions and carefully listening to whatever she said, so desperate was I for the truth. Her information seemed quite credible to me since, having never seen Jeff or even a picture of him, she was able to describe him perfectly. She told me that Jeff was with Jesus, that he was happy and wanted to be there rather than here. He said to tell me, "Don't cry, Mommy; I'm happy." She assured me with authority that Jeff's spirit was with God before the car actually rolled on top of him, that he never felt the pain. I needed to believe that; I still need to believe that. She went on to explain that one day when I died I would see him again. I was encouraged and eager to learn more about an afterlife. Since the funeral director had referred to Jeff as a little angel, I started focusing on the possibility that there was a heaven. But, did everyone go there automatically? Although Betty led me to believe that, yes, everyone goes to heaven—or at least to the afterlife—she also believed in reincarnation, which meant that we keep coming back to live other lives until we get it right. I began to believe in reincarnation, but I was confused. If there was actually a good afterlife, why would anyone want to come back? According to what she said, my son was happy and didn't want to come back. I began to feel I was getting some deep understanding, but it was only the bare beginning. It didn't yet make sense to me.

I began delving into all sorts of occult practices, soaking up any information that anyone had, from having my astrological chart examined, to learning about numerology, to having my palm read and my handwriting analyzed—all activities that God calls abominations *(see Deuteronomy 18:9-14)*. Because the big interest at that time was reincarnation, there was much speculation about who we had been in past lives. It was easy pursuing these interests since several people on Bob's side of the family were involved in these things at some level. One night we even tried holding a seance to get Jeff to talk to us himself. I know now what a dangerous and foolish stunt that was, that demon spirits are the ones that show up at seances, but I longed to hear, see, or feel my son again. At the encouragement of the others, I almost—but not quite—convinced myself that he was there; I strained to feel the sensation of his little hand in mine.

Even stranger than the seance was my experience with a young man called David, so strange that I am not certain I can accurately describe what happened. I met David at a nearby pizza parlor where I was waiting for a friend. She was late and I was alone, so he eventually sat down at my table to talk. And wouldn't you know it, he was an expert on numerology. I, of course, was eager to hear anything he had to say and to have him "do" my numbers. As he did his calculations, a look of recognition appeared on his face, and by the time he had completed the process, he was excited and said to me, "It *is* you! You're the one I've come to help!" Can you imagine the effect that had on me? I really believed I was on a divine journey that night and the savior and helper who had been assigned to me had come. Now I would have all the answers. I was so excited! I met with him several times in my home; the conversations were so ethereal and bizarre that I can't describe them. The closest explanation I can offer is to say we played a lot of word games. He tested me a lot, told me what lives I had already lived and what I was to become, and talked a lot about his being a commander of some sort in God's army. One time he had me close my eyes and visualize a tree in front of me, then asked me to reach my arms out and put them around the imaginary tree. Once my arms were around it, he put his arms around me and the "tree." Since his hands barely met each other, he said he was just barely adequate to help me. It was weird. But did a red flag go up? Not yet.

I eventually met his girlfriend, Pepper, and we became friends. She alluded to the fact that he had had some mental problems, something about his frenetic energy, and had spent some time in psychiatric wards. They just didn't understand him, of course, so he had been subjected several times to being locked up and pumped full of lithium. Did I see a red flag yet? Not eager me; I just had compassion for him and believed that the world was missing the essence of this special, gifted man.

Did I see a red flag when I got a call from Pepper from the hospital one day, saying that David had been carted away from the pizza parlor and was again locked up? Somehow he had gotten his hands on a pitchfork (is that symbolic or what?) and had flipped out and attacked the customers, eventually running outside to protect himself behind a dumpster. Well, caring person that I was, I went to visit him in the hospital a few times and continued to spend time with this strange couple when he was released. They actually had me convinced that there was a deep spiritual significance to the song "Sergeant Pepper's Lonely Hearts Club Band," that Pepper had special powers, too. Was I gullible or just dumb?

David was at my house one day while my children were napping upstairs. He hadn't been there very long when he got very agitated and started yelling about something that made no sense to me whatsoever. I told him to be quiet and went up to see if he had awakened Shana and Robby. When I came back downstairs, he was in a strange squatting stance with his head in my fireplace, chanting something. If it hadn't scared me, I would have laughed. After a few minutes he got up, his face contorted, and began grabbing things from the mantel and throwing them down on the hearth. His actions and words were vicious and evil. I started yelling back at him, but I was scared. He was at least six feet, four inches tall, so he towered over me, and he looked like he wanted to kill me. Although I couldn't make sense out of most of what he said, I remember that he completely negated everything positive and complimentary that he had ever said about me, telling me now it was all a lie. I began to fear for my children. That "mother lion" instinct rose up within me and I took over, with a strength and forcefulness I would never have imagined, and I literally threw him out of my house, forever. I never saw or heard from him again. I didn't know anything about demons then, or the devil for that matter, but I know now that he was, in fact, demon-possessed. I saw and heard evil personified, its ugliness manifested before my eyes.

To me, the Seventies were an ugly follow-up to the flower-child, free-love, drug-induced Sixties. It seemed the hippies were desperately making an attempt to slide into adolescence. Bell bottoms were in style; perms for men were the craze; most of the music reflected the futility of the Vietnam War; free love pushed its way into the concept of open marriages and wife-swapping; and transcendental meditation was *the* way to find yourself. A young man who worked with Bob also tried to enlighten me through transcendental meditation (TM), but it didn't take me long to realize that he was more interested in my sexual fulfillment than my spiritual maturity. Of course, that wasn't hard to figure out after he told me that he and his wife had an "open" marriage and that she traveled on business often. No sense in his being lonely while she was away, right? His guidance did not have any effect on me since I was not about to empty my mind and start chanting for anyone. Thank God for His protection in this situation and for the good common sense with which I was born; this was one situation in which I actually exercised it.

Ironically, although these were ungodly pursuits and I was setting myself up for deception and possibly worse, it was through this process that I started having an awareness of God, that possibly He was putting things in my path to give me an awareness of Him. To reflect back on it now, I can see His hand of protection on me the entire time. I gleaned just enough out of each experience to encourage me to continue, but each door closed before I was harmed in a significant way or completely misled.

Although it would seem our little family should have been happy and settled now, we were not. Since I have no intention of maligning Bob's character through this writing, suffice it to say that he moved on to greener pastures. We were divorced by the time the children were three and eighteen months old, respectively. Many of the strange experiences I have related took place after we were separated, when I was alone, lonely and vulnerable, and desperate to find answers. Bob never seemed to share my need to understand Jeff's death, so I pursued it on my own.

I was beginning to feel like a jinx with men. Here was another man who stopped loving me and left, pretty much humiliating me in the process. We had gone through so much together and I thought he was the love of my life, but, just like my father, he walked away. What a waste that he had left his first family for me and then left me for someone else. Except for our children, I felt like our time together had been useless. So many people had been hurt because of us, and then we couldn't even make it work. One would think that sharing the death of our child would have bound us together inextricably, but perhaps it became a wedge of unresolved hurt between us. During one of our last conversations before he was gone from our home, Bob commented that, tragically, it might have been different if Jeff had lived. I doubt it, because he followed that statement with another that took me years to forgive, and I still can't comprehend how he could have said it. When I reminded him that we had two beautiful children that were alive, he said that he had proved to his dad that he could father another boy, and now that part of his life was over.

I think it's important to note that I knew from a dream that he was going to leave me for another woman, maybe even before he did. Whenever I have had prophetic dreams, I have awakened with a distinct physical sense that I have witnessed something that is going to change my life. Such was the case this time. The dream, although difficult to describe in words, was very clear to me. As Bob pursued another direction, his body began to fade, as if he were becoming transparent. I heard a voice saying, "He is going to leave you." In the dream I shot him in the head before his body had totally disappeared. Killing him wasn't prophetic, per se (he is still alive), but later when he and I counseled with a psychologist, I was told that my action was accurate, that his problem was in his head: his thought patterns. I didn't tell Bob about the dream until after his extramarital relationship was out in the open; when I did, he was truly afraid of me for a while. I enjoyed his fearing me, since he was usually intimidating and because I had very little power in anything concerning him.

So, here I was, totally alone with two babies, feeling ugly and unwanted again, a total failure at marriage, and a failure as a person. Although I had failed motherhood the first time, I knew that wouldn't happen again; I had been given a second chance. Shana and Robby were the only reasons for me to live. So many have asked how I got through it all (including things I didn't write about)—wasn't it hard with two babies to take care of? My response was, Is breathing hard? They were my life, a gift to me, and being their mother was the only thing I knew I was destined for. Even Bob had often told me I was an excellent mother.

Although I was on an even keel with my children, I was at rock bottom emotionally. During the last months with Bob, I had lost a lot of weight and continued losing when on my own. My weight edged toward what I had weighed as a preadolescent, and my doctor was shocked the first time he saw me that thin, since I had been overweight all the time he had known me. After examining me, he determined that I was actually very healthy, "just miserably unhappy," which led me to ask myself questions about my life. Why was my life going so badly? What was wrong with me that I kept ending up alone? For a reasonably smart person, why did I keep making such foolish choices? Who was the real Sharon? Had they stopped loving the real me or the someone I thought they wanted me to be? I had no answers to these questions, so I decided that I needed to find out who I was and if there were, indeed, major character flaws that had to be fixed. I could not go on with life as I knew it.

Even though much of my life I had felt alone, this was actually the first time in my life that I had to live alone. I had my children, of course, but no other adult. I had gotten used to Bob's not being there most of the time, but now it was definite; he would never be coming home again. It was a little scary at first, but I soon realized what a relief it was. No longer did I have to worry about when, or if, he was coming home, if he would have lipstick on his shirts (I know, how cliché, but it really happened), as well as the scent of perfume (and I knew whose perfume it was), or if he would still be damp from his recent shower. A friend once told me that if a man would leave someone for me, he would leave me for someone else. And there it was! Now it was someone else's turn to worry about his staying faithful.

When he first began asking for a divorce I refused to give him one because I knew it would make Gwen, the other woman, really angry. After adjusting to my new sense of freedom, however, I decided that I needed to rid myself of the excess baggage. Keeping someone attached to me who would never be mine was only hurting me. Interestingly, when I told him to go ahead with a divorce, he cried. Shana says that she, as a two-year-old, can remember this conversation. I can see it now, as we sat at the dining room table and watched Robby, our beautiful, curly-headed baby, toddling around and playing with our dog as Bob seemed to be calculating his loss. For that moment I had the upper hand; I had taken control of my life and it felt good. I believe I was ahead of him emotionally at this point. I had mourned the loss of our relationship until I had no tears left, and now it was time for me and my children to make a life for ourselves.

6

Paradigm Shift

I had a terrible scare on Labor Day weekend of 1973. Shana was spending the weekend at Grandma and Papa's house in San Jose, and Robby and I were home alone in San Mateo. He was fifteen months old.

It was late afternoon and I was frying chicken in an electric frying pan, watching and turning the pieces as I also washed vegetables for a salad. Robby walked in behind me, grabbed the cord on the pan, and pulled it off the counter. A pan full of hot oil and chicken poured out over his head and down the front of him. Pure reflex action took over and I hit the pan with my fist, trying to deflect it from him. Fortunately, he was wearing a long-sleeved shirt and long pants, but the boiling oil still went through the fabric. You can imagine his piercing screams. I called his doctor, then raced my screaming child to the hospital. It was a nightmare. Here I was in an emergency room again with a severely injured child, whom they had to sedate to be able to examine and dress his wounds. I talked and sang to him the entire time, watching everything they did to him, almost coming apart when they splinted his little arms so that he wouldn't be able to touch his face. By the time they finished, the sedative had fully taken effect and he was asleep. Since his room in Isolation was not yet ready, I sat there holding and rocking him, finally breaking down into hysterical sobbing, feeling so guilty that I had let this happen. What kind of mother was I? Were my children not safe with me? The old guilt about Jeff's death, which still clung to me like a heavy cape draped around my shoulders, clutched me once again. But from somewhere deep inside came the assurance that Robby was going to be fine; I never feared that he would die.

The doctors' biggest concern was for Robby's eyes, which were blistered and appeared to be burned shut. Late that night, after he was settled in what was to be his room for the next five days, a husband-wife team of ophthalmologists came to examine his eyes, and their report was encouraging. The oil had apparently not penetrated the actual eyeballs. At least that was a relief.

Bob had arrived by that time, so we tucked Robby in his temporary bed and very reluctantly left for the night. Once in the parking lot, Bob let loose on me: How could I let this happen? Didn't I realize that he was packing for a trip in the morning and that driving from Hayward (where he was living with Gwen) to San Mateo was a terrible inconvenience? How did I think we were going to pay for this? He might as well have run me over with his car. I drove home sobbing again, filled with hatred for him and with guilt that my baby was lying in a hospital room, hurt and alone. Although I was exhausted physically and emotionally, I knew that sleep would elude me that night. When I got home, I faced the fried chicken mess in the kitchen, noticing that I had hit the electric pan so hard that the legs had broken off.

I got through that night and the next day and the next, spending entire days with my boy, entertaining him as best I could. I brought toys and things from home that could be sterilized, and I had to wear a sterile gown and mask. The most important item I brought from home was his blanket (his "badoodoo"), which he used when sucking his thumb. The splints on his arms thwarted his getting his thumb to his mouth, but I figured having his own blanket would help. I had no idea what sterilizing would do to it (they apparently saw no need for fabric softener). He literally had to bend it so he could cuddle with it. What a drag—stiff arms and a stiff blanket!

Through it all, Robby was a trouper and such a little charmer that by the second day he was the darling of the entire ward. Even nurses who weren't actually caring for him doted on him, donning gowns to play with him, bringing him little treats, extra juice, or just stopping by to see how he was doing. Although I had to hold back tears each night as I left for home, I was comforted by the loving care he was receiving.

By the end of the week, however, Robby had had enough of this inactivity and incarceration. By the time I got to the hospital the day before he was released, he was sitting in his bed, which he'd torn apart, the splints were ripped off, as well as his diaper, and he was playing with the little pellets that he had produced in his diaper. I guess you would call that resourceful! There was a window in his room that looked into the room next door, and the family of the child in there had been watching him and laughing.

His dad went to the hospital with me to bring him home, and once home Bob decided to take pictures of our scabby, scarred son. Although he was still a mess, he had improved considerably during his hospital stay. The prognosis was that he would have scars but at least no permanent damage to his eyes. I refused to accept that, so although I had not yet forgiven God, I began to pray for my child every day. Even though I believed that He hadn't answered me for Jeff, I somehow was trusting that He was listening to me now. And, amazingly, each morning when I went into Robby's room—he always stood up in his crib and called for me when he woke up—he was noticeably better. As the scabs fell off, beautiful new skin was there. In a short time he was completely healed, without a trace of scarring. I was not cognizant of it at the time, but my praying was a small step of faith for me that led me down a new path. Instinctively I knew that my son needed supernatural help and recognized that God could give it. It was the blind-faith cry of a mother's heart interceding for her child. And He answered.

My softening toward God was only one of the changes occurring in me during that time. I had survived this ordeal with Robby, I was managing a home on my own, was becoming strong with a new kind of independence, and was feeling in control of my life. As I saw myself through new eyes, I recognized my strengths and began to like the "real" Sharon. As I analyzed my life and my two failed marriages, quite an accomplishment for someone still in her twenties, it was a revelation to me that I had not been the partner with the problems. All I had ever wanted was to be a wife and a mother (and a teacher) and to have male approval and companionship, but I went about it in the wrong way. I got into the first marriage because of a lack of courage on my part, being afraid to say "no," even though I knew it was wrong for me. Bob showed up and harvested a fruit ripe for the picking. Although I am certain he had no idea of how entangled we would become, he inadvertently filled many of my needs: he was older by ten years, charming, loving, eager to build up my self-esteem, and willing to sacrifice for me. I believed that I could change the patterns of his life and that I would be enough for him. I am not saying that I am without fault, obviously, since most of this book depicts my weaknesses and failings, but I believe that my major contribution to the destruction of these marriages was my negative reactions to the bad behavior, which exacerbated the problems.

Another relocation brought about more changes in me. San Mateo was too expensive, so Bob moved the three of us to San Jose just days after Robby was home from the hospital. Moving day was Saturday, September 15, 1973, which was also the day of my class reunion, for which I had paid and looked forward to going. As I glanced around our new rental home filled with unpacked boxes, I now admit to indulging in a heavy dose of self-pity. How different my life had turned out from what I had imagined. I was disappointed I would have to miss the reunion, but with no date, no husband, a baby just out of the hospital, and not even one box unpacked, it was obviously out of the question. On the list of my life's priorities, the reunion took a nose dive to the bottom.

Once we were settled, divorce proceedings began. Since Bob has a law degree, he took care of preparing and filing the papers; it was relatively painless. I got full custody of our children, so I was relieved about that. He pushed me to get a job, but I flatly refused, saying something to the effect that if he was going to play, he was going to pay. I would not leave my children to go to work because he decided to be somewhere else. During the next few years we had many differences of opinion, several of which became legal issues, but with my new-found assertiveness and confidence I fought for what I felt was right—and won. Bob told me he was surprised that I had fared so well, commenting that he never thought I would make it on my own.

I spent so much time at home with my children that Grandma and Papa started encouraging me to go out, saying I was too young to be stuck at home all the time. I did date some, men referred by friends or family, but the majority of them acted as if I were the desperate divorcee waiting for some wonderful man to ease my loneliness. The lines sounded like dialogue from a bad "B" movie. It was more fun and safer to be with Shana and Robby.

Bob's first wife, Evelyn, and I had become friends by now, spending time together, watching each other's children, and even double-dating with men that she knew from work. We laughed about starting our own club, the "Ex-Wives of Bob" Club. Since we had the same last name and slightly resembled each other, we were often asked if we were sisters. Yes, we were sisters by marriage.

As I spent time at Evelyn's house, I eventually noticed one male friend of hers who was often there fixing things. He never talked, just stayed in the background painting or hammering. She introduced him to me and explained that George was a single man from work whom she dated occasionally, usually when they both wanted to go somewhere but didn't have a date. He had been a good friend, always willing to help out with household repairs. He was nice but extremely quiet.

I never paid much attention to him until Thanksgiving of that year, when Evelyn invited both of us for dinner, along with other friends. Because he was so shy, I felt sorry for him and pursued a conversation so he wouldn't feel left out. I even commandeered him into doing the dishes so that Evelyn could visit with her friends over dessert. He was a little more talkative when a chore was the focal point, and I found out that he too had lost a son, his second of four boys, who drowned when he was seven. That was an unfortunate thing to have in common, but it created a kind of bond of understanding.

George took an interest in me after that, even working up the courage to call me. The first time he came to my house, he had a carton of Pampers, which I thought was a little strange but a thoughtful idea. He knew I had little money, they were on sale, and he wanted to help. I thought, What a nice guy. As we talked that evening, he commented that he had never talked to anyone so much in his life, that no one had ever really listened. As you might guess, I couldn't get rid of him after that.

I did go out with him, but I was torn between his being a nice guy and being very far from what I thought was my type. He clearly thought I was the best thing since peanut butter and seemed so honored that I would go out with someone like him, often using the phrase "beauty and the beast." I didn't want to hurt his feelings, so I didn't send him away, and I actually began to feel safe with him. He was very good with my children, who were only three and eighteen months old respectively, so that had an effect on me. As he became serious about our relationship, to the point of talking about marriage, he often said he wanted a second chance to be a father. While I took that as a positive comment, since single mothers with small children do not often see themselves as marketable, in retrospect I should have seen it as a red flag. Why did he need a second chance? What happened with his first children?

But here I was again, seeing a way to fill a need. My children needed a father, I needed help financially, and here was a man who practically worshipped me, willing to do anything I wanted. I saw stability and fidelity, that this person would never leave me for someone else. I did have feelings for him, but I can't honestly say I was in love with him. I had compassion for the hurts he had suffered, so I was willing to try to be a source of healing. We decided to elope on Jeff's birthday to Reno, which we did, taking along some family members, including Evelyn, as witnesses. The night before, however, my instinct told me to call the whole thing off. Was God trying to warn me? I should have listened, but once again I was too weak to say no, and it was a decision with consequences my children and I would suffer for sixteen years.

In Chapter Ten I will give an overview of what our life was like. The actual end of that life is another incredible story of God's mercy and powerful hand on my life, as my children and I were divinely rescued, relocated, and healed.

7

Rescued

My five-year-old Shana came home one day after playing with Tanya, a four-year-old who lived across the street, and asked me who Jesus was. I knew that her family went to a Baptist church and that they called themselves Christians, but I didn't really know what that meant. I didn't have an answer for Shana about who Jesus was. The only thing I knew about Him was the song "Jesus Loves Me," which we had sung in Sunday School as children, but no one ever told us who Jesus was or why He loved us.

Michele and I had gone to Sunday School occasionally as children, usually at the church closest to our home. My mother made us go but did not attend church herself, except for an occasional program in which we sang with our classes. We never understood why we had to go and she didn't, and why she forced us to go when we didn't like it. During the summers in Hollister with our grandparents, we had to go to the Presbyterian church with them, but it was extremely boring and the music was suitable for a funeral. We had actually both been sprinkle-baptized as babies in that church, although no one ever explained the significance of it. Actually, the only significance it probably had was that it was traditional. I don't believe, at least as far as my family was concerned, that there was any spiritual purpose attached to it.

I do remember memorizing John 3:16: *"For God so loved the world that He gave His only begotten Son, that whosoever should believe in Him, should not perish but have everlasting life."* Unfortunately, no one explained what it meant. We, in fact, memorized many verses but were never taught their meaning. Now my child was asking me about the Son of God, and I had no answers.

I felt a little frantic about this new development, since Bob had by this time married Gwen, who was Jewish, and he had converted to Judaism. They were sending my children things pertaining to their religion and I was not amused. I had no idea about the validity of Judaism, but because it was her religion I had no intention of allowing my children to be influenced by it in any way. (She will probably never know that she helped push me in the right direction.) It just so happened that George's mother and sister had started attending a church that they were really enjoying, which was saying a lot since none of us to that point had any interest in church at all. It was June of 1976 now, seven years after Jeff died, and I still had not forgiven God for taking my son.

But suddenly I had a need to go to church. I decided that I would be a better example than my mother and actually stay in church with my children; they would go to Sunday School and I would be in the church service. I had no idea what I was getting into.

Right away I noticed the music, which was nothing like the boring hymns of my childhood. The words seemed to speak to me personally, as if someone had read my mind, and the melody melted my heart and made me cry. I had no idea why. The people were happy and excited, and it all seemed to center around this person, Jesus. The message was contemporary and actually understandable. I saw my first baptism by immersion, which at first I thought was weird, until I saw the radiance and joy on the face of the person being baptized as he came up out of the water. The children loved Sunday School and wanted to go back each Sunday. This was truly culture shock for me, but I was touched in a way I had never been before, though I did not yet understand it. It made me very quiet and reflective each Sunday as we went home, as I tried to absorb what I had heard and seen. George was going, too, and also seemed to be processing in his own way, not wanting to discuss his feelings.

It didn't take very long for me to get the message of the scripture I had known all of my life: that God loved us so much that He sent His only Son, Jesus, to be sacrificed so that we could go to heaven and have eternal life with Him. There it was, the way to get to heaven—the answer I had been pursuing for seven years. I had explored many options, but somehow I knew that this was the truth. I came to understand that to get to heaven you had to be "saved," which meant that you had to believe in Jesus as the Son of God, that He came in the flesh and died and rose again, and that you had to ask Him into your heart. Like a light going on, I realized that Christianity was not a religion per se, but a relationship with God Himself, made possible by His Son, Jesus. Jesus said, *"I am the way, the truth, and the life. No one comes to the Father, except through Me"* (*John 14:6*). I had suspected, but now it was confirmed, that people do not just automatically go to heaven. It does not matter whether they have lived a good life or not, everyone must make the choice. Everyone, that is, when they are mature enough to fully understand what it means. I understood that small children who are not capable of fully understanding and making that choice—who have not yet reached an age of accountability—are automatically taken to heaven when they die.

But, if we had to be "saved," what were we saved from? If God had seen such a tremendous need that He sacrificed His Son to accomplish it, then what He saved us from must be pretty terrible. I thought back to what Betty (remember, the psychic?) said about Jeff being in heaven—actually his spirit—and I understood that in reality only our physical bodies die, while our spirits live on forever. If being with God in heaven meant eternal *life*, then not being in heaven must mean eternal *death*.

Hell was created for the devil and his demons, who were originally created as angels. The devil, whom we call Satan (meaning *adversary*), was originally named Lucifer (meaning *light-bearer*), and the Bible says he was the most beautiful angel. Being too full of himself, he made himself equal to God, so God threw him and his loyal followers out of heaven. They literally went from the light to darkness, from good to evil, from love to hate, from reward to punishment. In God's own words from Isaiah 14:12-15,

> *How you are fallen from heaven, O Lucifer,*
> *son of the morning! How you are cut down to*
> *the ground, you who weakened the nations!*
> *For you have said in your heart: 'I will ascend*
> *into heaven, I will exalt my throne above the*
> *stars of God; I will also sit on the mount of the*
> *congregation on the farthest side of the north;*
> *I will ascend above the heights of the clouds, I*
> *will be like the Most High.' Yet you shall be*
> *brought down to Sheol [hell], to the lowest*
> *depths of the Pit.*

You can see why Satan and his demons are God's enemies and why they would do anything to keep people out of heaven and away from serving God. Satan wants the power and attention, wants all to worship him instead of God, which means that the more people he can pull away from God, the more company he will have in hell. Who do you think dreamed up the idea of reincarnation? The Bible says, "*Man is appointed ONCE to die, and after this the judgment*" (*Hebrews 9:27, emphasis added*). If you look at this from the devil's perspective, you can see how effective it is: convince people that they have other chances to get right with God, that if they mess up now they can come back in another life and try again.

Satan has many other names that depict his evil acts, one of them being the "father of lies." I recently heard someone say that the greatest lie the devil has perpetrated on mankind is that he doesn't exist. Remember David in an earlier chapter? I am absolutely certain that David was assigned to me by the devil. I was desperate for answers; I already had what were identified then as psychic abilities; I was gravitating toward anything that pertained to the occult, so I was a prime prospect. Do you think it was a coincidence that he just happened to be at the pizza parlor that night, that he brought up numerology, that he said he was "sent to help me?" He and his girlfriend were not even from that area. Even the pitchfork ties in. I know that he was demon-possessed; the evil I saw manifested was real and terrifying.

In January of 1997, we hosted a dramatic presentation at our church called The Glory and the Fire. It graphically depicts heaven and hell, angels in heaven, and the devil and his demons in hell. The drama consists of several typical-life scenarios, but in each the players die. In each scene, the characters are told about Jesus, that only those who call upon His name will be saved, and their names are entered into the Book of Life. After death, they find themselves at the entrance to heaven, facing a host of angels and a chief angel standing at a podium with a large book from which he reads. Each person has an instantaneous revelation of where he is headed. How tragic that they had not listened and taken seriously the warnings they had been given. Their final destination is known as they ask if their names are in the Book of Life. Those whose names are not found inscribed there are dragged off to hell, while a screeching, hideous, gloating Satan laughs that his tricks have worked, his lies have been believed, and now they are fully his forever. It was very powerful for the audience, and many people got saved; moreover, many who had turned away from God rededicated their lives to Him. This kind of up-close-and-personal presentation makes clear that a decision for God is what determines a future of eternal life.

What is the Book of Life? The name of everyone who has been saved is written in the Book:

*But there shall by no means enter it anything
that defiles, or causes an abomination or a
lie, but only those who are written in the
Lamb's Book of Life. (Revelation 21:27)*

*And I saw the dead, small and great,
standing before God, and books were opened.
And another book was opened, which is the
Book of Life, and the dead were judged
according to their works, by the things which
were written in the books. And anyone not
found written in the Book of Life was cast into
the lake of fire. (Revelation 20:12, 15)*

And what about "the judgment?"

*For we must all appear before the judgment
seat of Christ. (2 Corinthians 5:10)*

*And there is no creature hidden from His
sight, but all things are naked and open to
Him to Whom we must all give an account.
(Hebrews 4:13)*

I learned more about heaven: You not only get to go there,
but the moment you get saved all your past sins are forgiven. That's
what being born again means! That you are literally given new life, a
clean slate, as it were: *"Therefore, if anyone is in Christ, he is a new
creation; old things have passed away; behold, all things have
become new" (2 Corinthians 5:17)*. Not only are all sins forgiven,
but they are forgotten by God. Spiritually, you can no longer be held
accountable for them because they have been erased. I certainly had
things in me that needed changing and had done things that needed
forgiving. I did not want to look forward to punishment.

There was even more. I heard that God was our heavenly
Father and that He wanted us to recognize that and be His children,
to come to Him with the same kind of trust as children have for their
natural parents. Jesus said in Mark 10:15, *"Assuredly, I say to you,*

whoever does not receive the kingdom of God as a little child will by no means enter it." Even though trying to capture that kind of childlike trust was a stretch for me, deep down I really wanted a father I could trust, one who would love me just the way I am and never leave me, one who would protect and help me so that I wouldn't have to do it alone any more.

As wonderful as all of this sounded to me in theory, this new concept of totally giving my life in absolute trust to Someone I couldn't see scared me. What changes would I have to make in my life? Would I have to give up what little fun I had? Would all my family and friends think I was weird? What if I got sent to Africa to be a missionary? No one I knew except Carole was a Christian, so I had no one close by (Carole lived in southern California) for support or understanding. And I hadn't been too sure about Carole. When I had heard her talk about praying for people, I thought it was weird, a waste of time, too much "goody two-shoes" stuff. Bible verses like the following at first scared me, then drew me in as I weighed the importance of life's priorities:

> *Then Jesus said to His disciples, "If anyone desires to come after Me, let him deny himself, and take up his cross, and follow Me. For whoever desires to save his life will lose it, but whoever loses his life for My sake will find it. For what profit is it to a man if he gains the whole world, and loses his own soul? Or what will a man give in exchange for his soul?"*
> *(Matthew 16:24-26)*
>
> *The thief [the devil] does not come except to steal, and to kill, and to destroy. I have come that they may have life, and that they may have it more abundantly. (John 10:10)*

What I understood from these verses was that I had to give up the control, that is, living a God-centered life instead of a self-centered life. In doing so I would not only gain eternal life, but my life here on earth would be fuller, more productive, more joyful. That does not mean that we never have problems, which I certainly have found out through the years, but we can perform better in the problem situations. Through prayer, external issues can change or disappear. But even when they don't, we can become stronger through the process of dealing with them. With God as your dad, how can you lose, no matter what the outcome to the natural eye?

I understood that God has a distinct purpose for each one of us, and, by my choosing to do things His way, He would be able to accomplish that special thing that He created me to do. So far, my being in control of my life hadn't been too successful. And really, what did I have to lose? From my outward appearance people thought I had it all together, never knowing what anguish, unrest, and guilt still languished inside me like a stagnant pond. If the only benefit in my giving myself to God was to get to heaven, then I would have accomplished what I had set out to do. I knew where my son was and that if I made the choice, I would be with him again one day.

I decided I needed this relationship with God, and I knew that it would take a great amount of faith to follow through. I let two or three Sundays in church go by without going forward to make my life-changing commitment, keeping a white-knuckled grip on the back of the pew in front of me. I felt like I was in a tug of war—the spirit was willing, but the flesh was weak. Finally, however, toward the end of July of 1976, with knocking knees I went forward to accept Jesus as my personal Savior (as did George). It was a most amazing experience; I was truly changed on the inside. I felt like the weight of the world had been lifted off my shoulders; an unexplainable happiness just bubbled up inside of me. On August 31, I was baptized by immersion (the way Jesus was baptized), and that too was an awesome experience, something you have to experience to understand. Within the next few months, my children also asked Jesus into their hearts and were baptized.

Carole was the first person I called with the good news; she was beyond excited. It was then that I found out that she had been praying for me for ten years! She said that through all the things that had happened during that time, she saw (sensed) God just hovering over me, protecting me, gently guiding me through situations that ultimately led to a recognition of Him. There were so many times that she would pick up the phone to call me, to comfort me, to try to share Jesus with me, but each time she felt God telling her, "No, leave her alone, she's Mine, let Me do it." Because she was obedient to that, I can look back and see God's hand on me the entire time, as if He had been dropping bread crumbs for me to follow. Although this was only a glimpse, I was beginning to see that He had been there all the time. However, I had yet to put all the pieces together as they related to my son's death.

Carole began to teach me via long distance: phone calls, notes, scriptures, sermon tapes by mail. I was the proverbial sponge, soaking up everything I could get my hands on, establishing a daily prayer time and a Bible study time, and I began memorizing scripture. I was amazed at how alive the Bible was, discovering that I could read a verse (Psalms became my favorite book) one day and get one meaning, but on another day it would say something else, each time giving me just what I needed. Those verses expressed emotions in words far more eloquent than mine. I became like an excited child as a whole new world opened up to me. Being a new Christian is like child birth; you have to experience the miracle of new life before you can really understand.

8

Revelation

When Shana and Robby were about to enter second and first grades, respectively, we decided to enroll them in the Christian school run by the church we were attending. I had a day care business in order to be home with my children, but it was not very lucrative, so I chose to go back to work to pay for their education. I had not worked outside the home in eleven years, so this was a challenge for me. However, it didn't take long to get a job that was a perfect placement for me. I was hired as the church receptionist, which meant that my children and I would be in the same place all day.

Some time after I began working there, one of the pastors, Dave Jones, offered to lead a lunch-time Bible study for the secretarial staff once a week. Pastor Dave faithfully taught us for quite a long time, but there is only one lesson that I remember, because it put all the pieces of Jeff's life and death in place for me. It was an astounding revelation and the reason I was finally able to heal and offer this book as my testimony. As clearly as I can remember, this is the story he told that day.

In a country in Europe a long time ago, there was a man who worked as a draw bridge operator, which meant that he controlled the equipment that raised the bridge as boats and ships passed through the canal. It was a necessary procedure since the bridge hung relatively close to the water and ships could not pass through when it was suspended. Often his young son went to work with him, spending the day scampering among the woods and rocks in pursuit of imaginary outlaws or scaling the bridge trestle in an attempt to escape. He often climbed over and through the gears of the machinery that his father operated in order to raise the bridge. This he did against his father's stern instructions since the meshing gears and heavy equipment posed a danger. The boy also loved to watch the ships, destined for exciting adventures, filled with interesting and colorful passengers, many of whom waved as they sailed by.

Then one day the unimaginable happened. As a large ship approached and the man began to raise the bridge, he heard piercing screams coming from his son. In panic, he left his controls to find his son, guided by the sound of his terror and pain. He found the boy underneath the bridge, his body wedged in the metal, his arm trapped by gears. As he writhed in pain and pleaded for his father to pull him out, the man heard the ship's horn blasting, signifying its close proximity. What could he do? He would not be able to pull his son out without help and the ship, with hundreds of people on board, would crash into the bridge in a few moments, killing many of those hundreds of people either through the collision or by the sinking of the ship. With gut-wrenching anguish, he ran back to the controls and raised the bridge, sacrificing his only son to save those people. As the ship passed by and the people waved, they never knew that a precious life had been given for their safety.

Tears rolled down my cheeks as the impact of this story hit me. This father gave up his only son, letting him die an agonizing death, knowing that his father had chosen not to rescue him. What a painful and graphic picture of what our Heavenly Father did for us. He let His only Son die an agonizing death to save unloving sinners because He knew that would be the only way to their salvation.

No one at the office had known about the death of my son. Through my tears all I could say was "I know God's pain." In a moment I fully understood the price God had paid for me. Because He loved me so much, He had been willing to give up His Son to make a way for me to have a relationship with Him. He had allowed me to live through a graphic reality of what it had cost Him. As I sat there crying and trying to explain this revelation to everyone, I heard that inaudible voice again, saying, "Sharon, see what I did for you?" At times through the years when I have doubted that I mattered, that Voice has reminded me, "Sharon, see what I did for you?" He knows I know the agony of indescribable loss.

There was a long silence in that conference room as my story impacted Pastor Dave and the other secretaries. As I continued, I told them about Jeff, trying to articulate my thoughts as they came into my mind, speaking things I had never before realized. What kind of love does God have for us? Can any of us really understand the dimensions of it? I believe that I have a great capacity for love—I love thoroughly and tenaciously—but I can state unequivocally that I do not have the kind of love that would allow me to voluntarily sacrifice any of my children, including my stepchildren and grandchildren, for anyone.

While Jesus' sacrifice was God's plan, Jesus, in His deity, could only have been killed if He willingly gave up His life. He could have stopped the humiliation, the beatings, the crucifixion, but He came to fulfill His Father's plan, and in that He GAVE UP His life. There are verses that I had read in the book of John that instantly took on a different, more powerful meaning:

> *Just as the Father knows Me, even so I know the Father, and I lay down My life for the sheep. Therefore My Father loves Me, because I lay down My life that I may take it again. No one takes it from Me, but I lay it down of Myself. I have the power to lay it down, and I have power to take it again. This command I*

have received from My Father. (John 10:15, 17-18)

Greater love has no one than this, than to lay down one's life for his friends. (John 15:13)

In the days that followed, God began to show me all the pieces of my life and Jeff's that paralleled Jesus' own story. I am not equating my child or myself to Jesus and Mary, but I can see from God's perspective enough similarities for me to recognize what an awesome thing God has done in my life.

First of all, God gifted me in the prophetic (seeing things in the Spirit from God, either showing the truth about something already known or revealing something that is going to happen, which I will discuss later), and in His mercy He prepared me for what was to come. He told me that my child would "not live past the age of two." When I heard that Voice predicting my son's death, I believed it to be true since I had innately "known" things most of my life.

God prepared Mary for the conception, birth, and death of her son. She knew that her son was going to die an early death. To Mary was born a blessed child, and she knew from the beginning that God was entrusting her with a most glorious honor.

I, too, was blessed with a special child, and I feel tremendously honored by the privilege of caring for him, if only for a short time. I feel that God knew He could trust me to nurture him to accomplish the purpose for which he had been born. Going back to Hebrews 9:27, *"For man is appointed once to die. . . ,"* I believe that the beginning and ending of my son's life was set, that November 15, 1969, was his day to go home to be with the Lord, that no matter what I would have done with him that fateful day, he would have died.

Although growing as a normal child, just as Jesus did, Jeff showed an uncanny sensitivity and maturity in his attention to other people's needs. Remember, at the young age of twelve, Jesus taught in the temple.

I have read accounts and have heard stories about children who die and that somehow they sensed it and were prepared for it. I truly believe that Jeff knew, as best he could for a two-year-old, that something was going to happen to him. He was agonizing in those last two weeks of his life, just as Jesus agonized in the Garden of Gethsemane.

Jesus' death made a way for everyone who chooses to get to God, to have a personal relationship with him. It is my firm conviction that my son's death was the way God chose to get my attention, not only to give me an awareness of Him, but to make me desperate enough to seek Him out. He gave me strong survival instincts, optimism that there had to be a plan for this life, and such an incredible love for my little boy that I literally followed him right to God.

As soon as I could see much higher and farther than my pain, it began to make sense. I have heard it said that our lives are like a tapestry whose designer is God Himself. All we can see is the under-side, with all the knots and tangles of threads, while God sees the beautiful pattern that is being created. Where in the past I had been caught in the tangles of hurt, anger, loss, desperation, and failure, I was suddenly viewing the pattern God was weaving that represented my life. Woven into the fabric were experiences that, depending upon my reactions and choices, were designed to strengthen, refine, and prepare me to be what God created me to be, to accomplish the purpose for which I am here. My realization that God had been so intimately involved with my life showed me how much He loves me and how valuable I am to Him.

I finally realized that He wanted the best for me, that I was not being punished. He was bringing me up out of the grave to a new life, a new understanding, a new purpose. My search for answers had in large measure been completed and now it was time for the healing.

9

Healing

To everything there is a season, a time for
every purpose under heaven:
A time to be born, and a time to die;
A time to plant, and a time to pluck what is
planted;
A time to kill, and a time to heal;
A time to break down, and a time to build up;
A time to weep, and a time to laugh;
A time to mourn, and a time to dance....

Ecclesiastes 3:1-4

Jeff's seasons were few between the time he was born and the time he died, but his were woven into mine, his colorful threads winding through some of my greatest joys and very deepest sorrows. I can see the cycles of life bringing us full circle time and again—the time and circumstance appointed by God, the response ours. I had wept and mourned, I had been broken down, but I had survived. Now it was time to build, to laugh, to rejoice.

Healing begins with removing the burdens that cause us pain. Suppressing the memories or justifying their existence will not bring healing. The cliché "Time heals all wounds" is simply not true; a length of time will dim the memory, relegating the pain to a more inactive state, but it will not bring healing. In any circumstances or thoughts where pain surfaces, there are unresolved issues that need to be rectified. How do we do it? How did I do it? The answer is *forgiveness.*

"If you forgive the sins of any, they are forgiven them; if you retain the sins of any, they are retained" *(John 20:23).* Anyone whom we do not forgive stays tied to us, like being permanently handcuffed. There was a story on the evening news recently about a teenage girl who had gotten herself into trouble one too many times. The judge ruled that she must be chained to her mother 24 hours a day for several months. Christ died to *unchain* us from the past. Because of His sacrifice, we have forgiveness—the key that unlocks the chains—so that we can be reconciled to God. Because of the forgiveness we receive, we are able to extend forgiveness to others. As with the girl chained to her mother, once the matter was finished, the chains were removed.

As I focused on what God was showing me about my life, it became clear that my thoughts and feelings were constricted by anger, hate, guilt, sadness, pity, and layers of unforgiveness. I was compelled to strip myself of the garbage I had carried for so long, so I took action. I sequestered myself in my bedroom one afternoon and allowed the healing—the unlocking, as it were—to begin.

I got down on my knees by my bed and waited for Him to show me where to start. The beginning was the hardest—I had to forgive Him for taking my son. I confessed all my horrid feelings, pouring out my heart with words and tears, even saying the words, "I forgive you, Lord." That opened up the floodgates, as I wept so violently it was almost like vomiting. I began to forgive everyone I could think of who had hurt me and asked God to forgive me for all of the bad things I had done. And, just as important, I forgave myself. All the wrong choices had been mine, but if God had forgiven me and forgotten them, then I had to forgive myself.

And what a release—I had not killed my son! It was his time to die; nothing I could have done that day would have prevented it. Can you see God's mercy in preparing me? Can you see that I mattered so much to Him that he let me share His pain in losing His only Son, so that I would understand that He shared mine? Can you see that He did whatever it took to draw me to Himself? Can you really understand the *supernatural* work God has done in my heart for me to see and believe that God used my son's life and death to bring me to Him. . . and that I can thank Him for it? It is truly a miracle, for in my own capacity I could neither have accomplished this change, nor even imagined that it was possible.

As I have forgiven, relationships have been restored. Over the years, Bob has apologized to me, Shana, and Rob and has asked for my forgiveness a multitude of times. Bob has told our son that he feels lucky that he and Shana don't hate him. Well, the credit goes to him for not only pursuing forgiveness, but in establishing a relationship with his children. Of course his acknowledgment of his hurtful actions made him much easier to forgive. Bob divorced Gwen and married Darlene fifteen years ago, and together they have been wonderful to all of our respective children and kind and supportive to me as well. I appreciate them both. (And no, Gwen was not invited to join the "Ex-Wives of Bob" Club.)

About a year after Jeff died, I stopped going to the cemetery when I got beyond needing to talk to him there, his grave a grievous reminder of his physical death. After I became a Christian in 1976 and realized that my son was in heaven, I felt justified in staying away. During the writing of this book, however, I was strongly impressed by the Lord that I needed to go back there, that there was something unfinished. Sadly, I could not remember exactly what his headstone looked like. It had been 26 years since I had gone there, so pushing myself to do it was difficult. Finally one day, on the spur of the moment, my step-daughter, Amy, and I decided to go. It had just rained, so the skies were dreary and the ground wet as we drove onto the cemetery grounds. I located the vicinity where Jeff was buried, but we couldn't find his grave. We circled the area in the car and then got out to walk over the wet grass, wiping soggy leaves off little headstones trying to find my son. I started feeling very anxious and guilty that I couldn't find him, as if I had misplaced him. We finally had to go to the office and ask where he was, and, as the woman pulled out a card with his name on it, I started to cry. There was something so real and so painful about his name being on a card in a file in a cemetery office. Amy felt it too and cried with me.

When we located "Baby Land," just a little farther down than where we had originally looked, I knew right away by the trees that were still there just where his grave would be. I had to wipe off the marble of his small headstone, as it was almost completely covered with leaves, grass, and bits of dirt. Finally there was his name, the dates "1967 - 1969," and the bunny that I had chosen in November of 1969. Baby Land was different than before, more depressing because there were so many children buried there, all aged from two to five years, from what I saw. When Jeff was first there and I used to go sit with him, he was almost all alone, no one next to or very close to him then. In a strange way I ached because this place that had been the last connection with my son was sadly unfamiliar to me. I cried, of course, but it was a cry of acceptance and letting go. The Lord was right, I needed to go, and it finished something. I know now that I can go again to pay respect and to remember my baby, without the same anguish as before.

And the healing has continued, more in this past year than in any time since I have been a Christian. God has shown me things that I had buried, considered inconsequential to my life and too trivial to deal with. The writing of this book has been a tremendous catalyst for healing. I have prayed over every page of this manuscript, asking God to show me which stories to tell (believe me, this is *not* my entire life), and He not only has done that but has brought back a flood of memories totally forgotten. I cannot tell you how many tears have bathed these pages as I have mourned losses at every stage of my life. I had to relive the pain of Jeff's death and my life without him so that the reader could share my pain and understand how far I have come. As I have written about and become very angry at old, forgotten offenses, I have had to forgive and let go. It may be that if I had never written this book, I would have carried the weight of old hurts forever. My writing is as much for me as anyone who might read these words. *Nothing* is wasted in God's economy.

I have shared personal, embarrassing details about my life that I had kept hidden because I was ashamed. Through my transparency, God has shown me that there is no more shame attached to me, that these things are now permanently expelled to my forgiven past. The sharing of them was partly for me so that I could finally let them go, and partly for those who think they have been so bad that God couldn't possibly love them, use them, or change their lives. I am a walking testimony of a transformed life.

Much of this past year's healing occurred during our Wednesday night Bible study, which ended after fulfilling its eleven-month commitment. Our group was purposely small and closed, so it afforded relationship, accountability, and, above all, a safe venue in which we could allow God to work in and through us. I went into it asking God to clean out of me any old garbage, anything that was hindering me in my relationship with Him and others, anything preventing Him from accomplishing the purpose for which He had gone to so much trouble to save me. I asked Him to show me any blind areas, any weak spots that I might not be consciously aware of, since we cannot fix what we don't know is broken. Well, when you ask God to do something in you—and you mean it—you had better be prepared for change.

I had no idea that I was hoarding so many unresolved issues, but, as He showed me what was there, I acknowledged, I mourned, I confessed, I forgave, and I let go. He showed me that no wound is insignificant, no hurt too small to touch. He wants to take it all away.

A revelation to me this year was that any unhealed areas in us are targets for the devil to zero in on: to accuse or condemn us; to hang guilt over us like a black cloud; to make us think that God really doesn't care about us because He has allowed bad things to happen; to think we will never be good or clean enough to go to heaven; to keep us from reconciling relationships; to obliterate any hope for change; to keep us from our divine purpose.

As I went through this process, I realized that I was trusting God more than ever. The fact that I had let this group of people see my most private fears, failures, and feelings was a sign that I trusted the place in which he had set me. But, there was something that was still nagging at me, as if I were missing something, like trying to express a thought when the words won't come. I prayed and told Him that I wanted everything He wanted to give me, but the answer I got back was that I was not receiving. I did not understand that at all. I was doing everything I knew how to do.

The following Sunday after the morning service, the person sitting behind me stopped me to tell me something. I mentioned prophecy—the prophetic gift—earlier, and what he had to tell me was one such word. He said that God said there was some area of my life in which I felt incomplete, but that He was going to complete me. I didn't understand what was going to happen, but I knew that God had not just left me hanging out there with this nagging feeling. We were going all the way in the process of setting me free!

And it happened the following Wednesday night at our Bible study, which everyone in our group calls my "breakthrough" night. It was another one of those experiences that is hard to put into words. I became an object of show-and-tell as they watched the Lord miraculously release me from a burden and change me. During our lesson, I started answering a question, then I veered off in an entirely different direction, talking about what a graphic example of God's love had occurred in my life through my son's life and death. Let me interject something. Have you ever read or heard accounts of near-death experiences, where people are drawn toward a white light and see Jesus? In several that I have heard, each person states that Jesus communicated with them without words, that however He did it, they were able to understand Him and to respond with thoughts. My experience was like that. As I talked, He started communicating with me, and I realized that He was trying to tell me something. I stopped talking and listened.

In but a couple of seconds He showed me why I wasn't able to receive fully from Him. All of my life I had taken on the responsibility of caring for others, much of the time feeling guilty when things went wrong, even in situations completely beyond my control. Much of my burden was false responsibility that I need never have carried at all. In my mind, God had given me the responsibility of raising Jeff and in my mind I had failed Him because Jeff had died. I knew that I hadn't caused his death, but apparently somewhere deep inside I held onto a seed of guilt because of the way I had been patterned as a child. The reason that I was not receiving from God was not because I didn't trust Him, it was because *I* didn't trust *me*. I was afraid that if He gave me another precious assignment I would fail Him, so, subconsciously, I was resisting taking on anything of importance.

The group sat and watched this transformation—saw it on my face—as God gave me clarification, understanding, and release. In an instant He took it away. I could be trusted! I felt the weight of the world lifted off of me, and the burden disappeared. And, as you can guess by now, I cried. It was a miracle! I felt totally different, finally completely peaceful inside. Then, our group leader, Chuck, had a word of prophecy for me (although I can't remember all of it): "My daughter, the process is completed, the process is completed, the process is completed."

10

Triumph

I view the tapestry of my life differently now. I see it stretched across an embroidery hoop with the Master's hand lovingly and tirelessly at work. I cannot see the design from His perspective, as He looks down from above, but I can see the beautiful colors and the quality of the thread. His hand is steady and sure, each stitch deliberate and purposeful. As the Creator, He spoke the world into existence, and, in the same way, His Words—His stitches—give us life, form, and direction. No part of the pattern is abstract, just as no circumstances in my life have been coincidental. I believe He allows for a little slack here and there for the exercise of our free will, but when we pull and tug and try to create our own designs, we cause unsightly tangling. It is then that He patiently undoes the tangles, reties proper knots, and trims off the excess threads, alleviating needless bulk under the surface of the fabric. Sometimes this is a painful process, but it is imperative for the completion of the masterpiece.

I am now comfortable with the process, confident in His love for me and that He is accomplishing a purpose through all the phases of my life for which only I was created. It is not necessary that I understand it all for my faith to be strong. My faith has been built in my history. Actually, I realize that since my vision is limited and my human ways are so flawed and finite, it is useless for me to take total control of my life.

> *For My thoughts are not your thoughts, nor are your ways My ways, says the Lord. For as the heavens are higher than the earth, so are My ways higher than your ways, and My thoughts than your thoughts. For as the rain comes down, and the snow from heaven, and do not return there, but water the earth, and made it bring forth and bud, that it may give seed to the sower and bread to the eater, so shall My word be that goes forth from My mouth; it shall not return to Me void, but it shall accomplish what I please, and it shall prosper in the thing for which I sent it. (Isaiah 55: 8-11)*

God's Word is life-giving and purpose-oriented and as real today as any scripture in the Bible. He created humans in His likeness in order for us to be able to communicate and have a relationship with Him, so that we can hear and understand His Voice, and can actually talk to Him in prayer. And He intends that His Word will accomplish the purpose for which He speaks it.

Woven into a prophetic word is always a piece of information that only the person receiving would know in order to confirm that the message is truly from God. I have been blessed to have received prophetic words that have not only given me hope and direction, but which I have seen fulfilled in my life. You already know about God's telling me that my son would not live past the age of two, but there is so much more. I eagerly share with you some of the prophetic words given to me to show you how real and awesome God is. But first I must give the background.

My third marriage began in 1974 and ended abruptly at the beginning of 1990, when my children and I secretly moved out.

Although I will not describe the entire sixteen years here, I feel it is important to give you some of the history and the events that led up to our leaving.

What was at first a drawing feature soon became a curse, as George designated me for the proverbial pedestal, a place that is usually unrealistic and uncomfortable for the object of adoration. The biggest problem it created was that, until the later years, he would never argue with me directly since he didn't want to "rock the boat" of our relationship. So, if something upset him, he would take it out on Shana and Robby; he couldn't control me, but he had the upper hand over them. If he wasn't just grouchy with them, he would actually create and manipulate situations in which my children, no matter what their response, would end up in trouble.

It wasn't too bad at first when my children were very small and cute and too young to talk back, but, as they grew and their needs changed and interests broadened, he became more hostile because of the attention I gave them. In fact, he was jealous of anyone or anything that took my attention. So many social occasions were ruined by his embarrassing behavior (e.g. stomping out after some cruel remark, punishing the children in public because they were laughing too much, once throwing car keys at me at a wedding reception because someone asked me to dance, going into another room and refusing to talk to anyone). I eventually stopped scheduling anything, never inviting friends over. All my friends were at work. He was especially cruel to the children when I tried to be social in the evening with my friends. It finally wasn't worth worrying about what was happening at home, so I gave up trying to do anything social. We lived in virtual isolation except for dinners with family on holidays.

Carole and her family witnessed so many cruel and strange things that they felt uncomfortable coming to our house, but she never talked about it in detail until after the marriage was over. She watched my reactions and how I tried to smooth over the ugliness.

How can children understand that they will get scolded for having too much fun, for laughing too much? Much of the time we were walking on eggshells.

George was rigid in the things he considered important, either his method of doing things or his possessions: clothes, tools, magazines, car, even food, which he hoarded. No one else was to touch what was his. He was obsessive about his hobbies, almost like a religion. One Christmas he bought a basic train set and additional equipment to put together and add to the set. He said it was for the children, but they weren't allowed to touch any of it. When he was in a good mood, he would let Robby watch him paint train cars or little passengers, but Robby had to keep his distance.

His clothes were arranged by use and color, all his golf outfits were on single hangers—pants, shirts, and even the matching socks all layered together. He would *never* wear a pair of socks from one outfit with a different outfit.

No matter how well the children did in school or at sports, to him it was never good enough. He always demanded, "Well then, why didn't you. . . ?" He tried coaching one of Robby's little league teams but got fired from volunteering because of his temper. Whenever anything went wrong, he demoralized Robby in front of everyone. During a later season, an umpire actually stopped a game until George left the park because of his embarrassing and inappropriate reaction to a call.

Shana started out as a gregarious, self-confident little girl. But by preadolescence she changed to a shy, insecure, intense young lady. At night she would apologize for not being good enough that day, when she had been perfectly good. What power parents have over their children with the words they use. How sad that we can so readily absorb and believe the negative about ourselves.

Robby was always trying to get George to play with him or help him with "boy" things, but he was always sent away with, "I'm busy." "Busy" usually meant watching TV or reading a hobby magazine, *Golf Digest*, or *TV Guide*. Robby has never forgotten that and points to his self-sufficiency as the result. Whereas Shana grew increasingly dependent on me and very emotional, Robby, who was unfortunately like me in his self-reliance and suppression of his feelings, just went about proving he could do it and do a good job.

I believe that George's basic insecurity kept him from making decisions easily; he hated to be wrong and was unpleasant when he was. But once he decided something, nothing could change him from his self-appointed course of action. This was reflected on every vacation, making what was supposed to be the best time of the year a trial. He would figure out how much money we would need and never plan to get more should we run short. If we ran out, we didn't eat. There were two or three occasions when we arrived at Carole's a day or two early because we had no money to buy food. We arrived unannounced because he didn't want the expense of a long distance phone call. He always made a time schedule for driving, and if for any reason we got behind schedule, he would not even make rest room or food stops until we had regained our lost time. Try explaining that to two small children.

My nightly ritual was to spend quality time tucking in each child, trying to build back up, smooth over, explain injustices and irrational anger, and to let them know how much I loved them. It was our special time, and I know they remember it.

It was as if George had two sides, one a Casper Milquetoast and the other a raging tyrant. When set off, his angry words made no sense, so it was virtually impossible to argue and make him see reason. The things that set him off were very trivial, but I know that underlying those reactions was a desperately sick and wounded person. He always seemed to be in competition with Shana and Robby, and I remember asking him several times if he loved them, to which he answered, "No, I really don't." I told him our relationship would never work, that we would never be a family if that was how he felt. My children were a part of me; we couldn't be taken separately.

Often during the years after we had a bad day and I was trying to talk sense into him, I would suggest counseling. He would have none of it.

He changed his mind, however, when our marriage exploded in 1984 and I was almost at the point of having a nervous breakdown. George wanted counseling for us then and used the cruelest manipulation to get me to agree. He said that if I didn't try to put our marriage back together, God might kill my children. I did finally go but only to maintain my sanity and my hope that I would get a release from him. But we went to Christian counselors who would never recommend divorce, so I stayed and tried for another *six* years. Initially when our counseling sessions were over, he seemed better. But it was soon evident that the changes in behavior were not genuine. He tried to change the outward manifestations, but nothing had changed on the inside.

The last two years were horrible, as George focused on Shana as his target, becoming physically violent with her. Much of the cruelty was calculated to occur when I was not home, and then he would lie to me about what had happened. In his anger, however, he would forget about the friends who were in the house listening and seeing what he was doing. He actually told her she was the cause of all of our problems. When she would stand up to him and say that she was going to tell me, he would say, "Then you can just get out of this house and I don't care if you live on the street. And if your mother doesn't like it, she can get out too." Robby started catching him in the act and intervening on his sister's behalf. I came home to more than one occasion when Robby was going after George for hurting Shana.

During the last year, George and I were barely speaking to one another. When we did speak, it was usually an argument; at those times he told me the same thing he told Shana: "You can just take your kids and get out of here. I'm never leaving." He was staking his claim to the house. It was also during that time that he suggested we

have separate bank accounts and split the bill payment. I found out
soon after that he had written to all our credit card companies to
remove himself from the accounts, leaving me totally responsible for
the balances. He was apparently forcing an end to our relationship.

Desperate for some help, in November of 1989 I contacted a
well-known and respected counselor in our area, who was also a
member of the church I was attending at the time. (George and I
hadn't attended the same church for a long time; he rarely went at all
by this time.) I needed some resolution to this horrible mess and
tried once again to get help for George. He was resolved to
maintaining the status quo, having carved out his private universe in
the midst of three other tormented lives. He reluctantly agreed,
believing, I'm certain, that we would be encouraged to stay together.
It didn't turn out the way he expected.

Our counselor met with each of us individually, once as a
couple, and then gave us a battery of tests, including one set of
psychological evaluations. Another test we took twice, first answering
for ourselves, the second time answering as we thought the other
person would answer. It was geared to show how well we knew each
other. The results bore out everything that I had told the counselor.
George's psychological test showed two sides to his personality, with
a lot of pent-up hostility and anger. The other test, in which we
answered for each other, showed that I had him pegged perfectly,
while he didn't know me at all.

We met with the counselor one more time only, in which he
gave us the results of the tests and told us he would not counsel with
us any further. He believed that we did not belong together, that this
relationship was not going to be reconciled. Privately, by phone, he
asked me how we had ever gotten together in the first place. We were
absolutely mismatched, ill-suited, wrong for each other. He could not
understand how we had stayed married for so long, but, as a
Christian counselor, he could not actually recommend divorce. He
did point out that we were not Christians when we met and married,

so it was not a relationship that God had put together. And he was concerned for the safety of my children and me, feeling that a real explosion was imminent.

Another incident happened during the third week of January, 1990. Late in the day before I got home from work, Shana went into our room to use the telephone. He told her to get off, that she wasn't allowed to be in our room (his rule, not mine). The next thing she knew, he had grabbed her, shoved her up against his closet door and was threatening her with his fist in her face. Then Rob walked in. That was the final straw for him; he went after George. When I drove up, Shana ran out to the driveway in hysterics, yelling for me to get into the house. By the time I got inside, George was holding Rob down on the sofa, talking in his creepy, mock-reasonable voice, making it appear that Rob had been bad and George had used reason to calm down the situation. He obviously had heard me drive up, so he changed his course of action. He looked me in the eye and lied to me about what happened. Rob, who rarely showed his feelings, followed me to my room and broke down. He just couldn't stand it anymore. We couldn't keep living like this.

There was a service that night at my church that was a prelude to a prophetic conference coming the following week. I decided to go because I knew our counselor was going to be there and I wanted his advice. The children were terrified. I didn't want them to be home without me, so Shana went to church with me and Rob went to the neighbors' until we got home. When I spoke with the counselor, he told me to call the police and make a report, just to have it on file and to put a little fear into George. I never did call them, however, fearing retaliation from him. It proved not to be necessary since the next week was to be our last week with George.

Have you ever walked into a place that felt almost evil? That was the atmosphere of our house during the last year, but especially in the last week that Shana, Rob, and I lived there. I believe that for a number of years there was a demonic influence there, and the more involved I became in church and the more I prayed, the stronger the sense of evil. My children and I hated going home at night, as you can imagine from the events I have related. During the last year, the tension was so thick it was palpable. I felt that I was barely clinging to life emotionally and even told God more than once that I would rather die than continue to live the way I was. I actually carried in my mind a picture of myself on death row. I felt doomed and hopeless, as if I were waiting for the execution to take place. I never told anyone how desperate I felt, still trying to hide my problems. There were times when I felt I was losing my mind. My prayers were literally a lifeline for me, my only outlet for expressing my true feelings; God was the only One to whom I could bare my soul. And in 1990 He proved He heard every word, saw every tear, and knew every intimate desire and desperate thought.

A prophetic conference—or *presbytery*—is a time when a group of prophets ministers to select candidates, of whom they have no prior knowledge or familiarity. *"Do not neglect the gift that is in you, which was given to you by prophecy with the laying on of the hands of the presbytery" (1 Timothy 4:14)*. During the last week of January, 1990, there was such a conference at our church. Carole flew to San Jose to spend the week with me and to attend this conference, both of us praying that God would give me some direction as to what to do with my life. She immediately saw the tension in me and physically reacted to the atmosphere in our house. She watched as George talked to us through gritted teeth while clenching and unclenching his fists. Although I never told her the feelings I had about being on death row, nor that I was concerned about my "keeping it together" mentally and emotionally, it didn't take her more than five seconds to know that something— everything—was drastically wrong and that it was worse than she imagined.

We went to the conference expecting to receive something, but we had no idea how dramatic and personal it would be. During the first night of the conference, on Sunday, Carole and I were called out of the audience by one of the pastors who was ministering. He was about to minister to a couple, but he stopped and pointed to me where I was sitting almost in the back of the room. He said he could not continue until he had prayed for me, that it had bothered him all day, ever since he had first seen me that morning. He had never seen me before, didn't know my name or anything about me, but God had troubled him in his spirit until he had to take action. With legs trembling and tears starting to fall, we made our way to the altar, in awe that God had intervened to speak to me. I share that word here to show you that God knew everything.

> ...and there was a crushing effect in my spirit
> that's been there all day. It seems like you are
> waiting to be executed. It's just like an
> assassination that's taking place in your spirit
> and you have been going through agony,
> agony, agony, and it's been a prolonged thing.
> It just doesn't go one way or the other and you
> have been praying.
>
> I believe this is your girlfriend. The Lord
> showed me that one of the two of you was
> visiting here, and that both of you have been
> agreeing in the Spirit that whatever this
> problem is, it's going to come to the head. I
> don't know whether it's a husband or a child
> or parent, but it is a family matter—domestic
> matter very, very close to you. We are going to
> pray for you. Recently you have been fearful
> that you are even going to lose your mind,
> that you are going insane over the whole
> thing, that you are going to flip out and you've
> been walking right on the edge of the whole
> thing. But God says that you are doing great;

God says you are doing great. God is commending you for your faithfulness, coming and worshipping. Just by your general appearance, we wouldn't know, unless God revealed it; we wouldn't know there is anything wrong.

I have been wrestling with this all day. I said, "Well, Lord, she's standing there with her hands up, she's doing better praising than a lot of people that don't have any problems." And you are not going to lose your mind and you're not going to flip out. You are going to stay solid. This hope you have is an anchor of your soul. You are on the solid rock in the middle of the storm, my sister. You are anchored to Jesus and you will not be shaken.

Now, Father, in the Name of Jesus, we bind this thing right now. We pray, Father, that it goes one direction or the other. Father, this is what these two sisters have been praying for, that there would come a point in a place where there would be a direction. This thing would either clear up or go away. Now, Father, we pray that Your Great Will would be done and would bind the work of the enemy. We bind the assassination spirits, we bind the confusion spirit, these hindering spirits. There is an unclean spirit, it's not from you, but it's from the outside. Comes in and attacks. Father, we cast these things off her, the very influence they try to have on her, in the Name of Jesus. We charge them to loose their hold

*this very moment in the Name of the Lord Jesus
Christ of Nazareth.*

*May the Lord be exalted. I believe you can
walk out of here tonight triumphant. You are
going to go to bed tonight and you are going
to sleep like you have been drugged. Amen.*

Pastor Dave Hubert
January 28, 1990

On Wednesday of that week, the last day of the conference, I
was given a prophecy from another pastor, in which God gave me a
beautiful promise—that He was going to give me a brand new life
and that He was going to fulfill *every* area of my life. He also said that
my children and I would be so completely healed that there wouldn't
even be scars to see. As I heard these words, I saw in my mind those
prison doors on death row opening and that I was set free. I saw a
wide-open field, like a meadow, bathed in sunshine, and my sense
was that I had received a pardon—I was truly being given a new life.

By Thursday afternoon, after having lunch with our pastor's
wife, I felt the "release," that not only was I free to go, but that for our
safety, time was of the essence. It was clear to me that removing
ourselves from the household would be the equivalent of diffusing a
bomb. So, by the time my children got home that afternoon, I had
arranged for Shana to stay temporarily with a family from church and
for Rob and me to go to my sister's. My sister had quietly watched our
situation worsen, so she was relieved that we were making a move
and very willing to give us temporary shelter. Shana and Rob were
shocked when I told them what we were going to do, but then they
each took part in the preparation, simply trusting that I knew what I
was doing. They understood that I believed that God was letting us
go.

From that moment on, it was as though my seventeen-year-
old son became the man of our newly formed family. I was so proud
of the way he took charge, making quick and wise decisions, eager to

help and to protect his sister and me. He enlisted the help of some of his friends for the next morning and borrowed a truck, which he parked down the street from our house. Carole arranged to stay with us for another week, for which I will always be grateful; we couldn't have done it without her. Together, we four used the hour-and-a-half before George got home to plan, organize, pack things that wouldn't be obvious. . . and pray. I think we were all scared, but we had the determination to move ahead. Much like an army the night before a battle, we knew it was what we had to do. That evening the air was rife with tension, and we four were practically silent—partly not knowing what to say and partly afraid that saying too much would give away our secret. Shana and Rob spent most of the time in their rooms, certainly reflecting on the fifteen years they had slept there, and, in some way, perhaps, giving closure to their lives in that house.

I slept very little that night. When morning came I was alert to every sound as George went through his routine to get ready for work. I had not been sleeping in the master bedroom for some time, so my being sequestered in the spare room was not unusual. There was silence in the house until we were certain he had driven away. We cautiously filed into the hallway to coordinate our strategies. Then we went into action. By 4:00 p.m. that day, we were finished. Rob and his friends had completely moved all of Shana's possessions, storing some of them at a relative's and placing most of them in her temporary home. They had made runs to my sister's home with his things and mine, mostly our clothes and some personal things. I left behind all the furniture and other household items, taking only what was mine personally. I also left behind a four-page letter I had written, confirming that we had, indeed, left for good and explaining, if there was any doubt, why.

I finally talked with him about a week after we had moved, and he sounded very relieved that we were gone.

My children and I were relieved as well, but it was extremely traumatic ending a life and beginning another with such force; I believe we experienced a kind of culture shock. Although Shana was loved by and assimilated into her foster family, it was very difficult for her to be separated from us. I slid into "survival" mode emotionally, trying to adjust to my new environment, planning for the future and executing divorce proceedings, while still maintaining my performance at work and being some sort of security for my children. People watching me were waiting for me to crash and burn, but I never did. I had a difficult time sleeping, so in those quiet hours I prayed, reminding God of His Word to me that I would have an entirely new life and that *every* area of my life would be fulfilled.

As early as 1986, He started drawing my attention to a scripture, which promised me a restoration of things lost. When I first read it, of course, I had no idea how much loss my children and I would be experiencing. I also have "1988" written in my Bible next to those verses, so again He gave me the promise to sustain me as the years became more difficult. During those first three months of our new life, He brought it to my mind another time:

> So I will **restore to you the years** that the
> swarming locust has eaten. . . . You shall eat
> in plenty and be satisfied, and praise the
> name of the Lord your God, Who has dealt
> wondrously with you; and My people shall
> never be put to shame. Then you shall know. .
> . that I am the Lord your God and there is no
> other. My people shall never be put to shame.
> (Joel 2:25-27; emphasis added)

True to His Word, things happened quickly. By Mother's Day in May, I had gotten a new job and had bought a condominium, and the three of us were together again. I got a loan to buy new furniture and household items, so, except for Rob's bed, everything in our lives was new.

But that was only the beginning. Shana was blessed with the opportunity of spending five weeks that summer in Africa to play

basketball on a Christian team. Right after graduation, Rob was asked
to play on an all-star baseball team at a tournament in New York,
actually playing on the field at Cooperstown and touring the famous
museum there. Both of them were honored, and they experienced
things they will never forget.

I adjusted well to my new life. It was a tremendous pleasure
to have peace in my life instead of torment. It took me weeks after
moving out of our old house not to feel sick driving home at night,
but eventually I took joy each day in my new job and in going home
to a place of quiet and comfort. After three failed marriages, I
decided that I was better off alone. If God wanted me married, He
would have to bring the perfect person and prove it to me; I certainly
had no faith in my choices, nor did I trust men at that point. I dated
once—someone from my new company—but I felt uncomfortable.
There was much gossiping company-wide about almost any issue, so I
decided not to make myself a potential target. Anyway, my son, the
self-appointed man of the family, had laid down the rules for me: I
could not date anyone unless he met him first, and I could not have
sex with anyone I wasn't married to. He was rather protective, but that
was just fine with me! Actually, one of my biggest revelations during
this time was that I didn't *require* a man to meet my needs. I believed
that God had rescued me and He would take care of me.

Eventually, I did get lonely. My children were either out
much of the time or getting lots of phone calls when they were in,
and I realized that I had become socially-challenged. And I admit I
was even getting a little testy when none of the incoming calls were
for me. The day before Rob flew to New York for the baseball
tournament, however, he made a startling pronouncement: "Mom,
you should go out with Amy's Dad. Amy has been talking to him
about you. I've met him, and he's a really great guy. He comes to my
games sometimes. He works out and is good looking and has a good
sense of humor. We think you'd really get along."

"Amy" was Amy Gregory, the girlfriend of Rob's friend, Paul, whom I had met on several occasions. Other than a few brief conversations, I didn't know anything about her life, including the fact that she had a single dad. I was rather stunned that my protector was so ready to throw me at another man, not to mention that Rob had such a glowing opinion of him. My son is hard to impress and very reserved in making character judgments. That was Monday afternoon. By Tuesday afternoon, Paul stopped by my house to tell me that he and Amy had been telling Dennis, Amy's dad, all about me. Actually, his opening line was, "Did you hear about the match we made for you?" He tried to impress me with Dennis' working out, telling me how big he looked the first time they met. Dennis is only five feet, eight inches tall, so I guess his muscles looked very big to Paul. Amy, who was as protective of her dad as Rob was of me, apparently liked me, was giving her complete endorsement, and was encouraging him to call me—actually nagging him. I found out later that he was totally confused about what I was like: I was tall and small; I was 45 but looked 25. His only question was, "Is she boring?" when he found out that I was a Christian. They assured him I was not boring. He had been single for about five years, also planning to never remarry, happy with his sports, friends, and plenty of quiet time to read. He realized that he didn't *need* a woman to make his life complete. The real reason he called me on Wednesday evening was just to get his daughter off his back.

Dennis is not one to spend time on the phone unnecessarily, so he was amazed when our initial phone conversation lasted for twenty minutes. Rob was right; he did have a great sense of humor and was very easy to talk to. Before we hung up, he asked me out to dinner for the next night.

It was, for all intents and purposes, a blind date. From the kids' descriptions of us, we really didn't know what we were going to get. We weren't disappointed, in either appearance (he had even bought a new shirt for our date) or personality. We had a great dinner of Cajun food and a great conversation, which continued as we sat in his car for three hours after he drove me home. It never occurred to me to invite him in, but he didn't seem bothered by that. He kissed me and asked me out for the next week.

The rest, as they say, is history. He got attached to me very quickly, making it clear fairly soon that he loved me. I was much more hesitant, but the more I got to know him the more I appreciated the quality of his character, his unconditional acceptance of me, his understanding and compassion of what I had been through, and his recognition and appreciation of how far I had come. The more I saw, the more I listened, the more I trusted. I can say it unequivocally—and have many times—that he is the best man I have ever known.

Except for our tying up our respective phone lines almost every night, Rob and Amy were delighted with this match, for which they take full credit, and were very excited when Dennis asked me to marry him in March. We set June 1 as our wedding date. I loved this man and was happy, except for one thing: he was not a Christian. The Bible says not to "be unequally yoked together with unbelievers," so I worried that God might not be in favor of this match. I certainly did not want to make another mistake, so I prayed and asked Him. He answered me in a prophetic dream.

It was black at first, ominous and threatening, faintly-colored images beginning to form and swirl about. They were ugly and menacing and intending evil for me. I was shrinking back, crying, afraid, arms held up defensively in an attempt to protect myself. There was a sound, too, but one I can't describe other than it seemed demonic, the level increasing with the pace of the swirling images. It was very frightening.

Then it stopped. A Voice spoke: "Sharon, you will weep no more."

The black faded and light appeared on the horizon, such as the day dawning. It grew brighter and brighter until I could see the sun, very big and bright and almost eclipsing my visual range.

Then Dennis appeared in front of the sun, his handsome face smiling at me, as he got closer and closer. Then The Voice said, "I am giving him to you as a gift."

We were married on June 1, 1991, and it was about the best day of my entire life. Our wedding was just what we wanted—elegantly casual—and I felt a glow radiating from deep inside me that I had never experienced before. We knew that God had ordained our marriage and had blended the two of us together as one—a complete package. Although Dennis was not yet a Christian, I knew that day would come and that God would use me in his life to lead Dennis to Him.

When Amy, at 17, got pregnant, she became very interested in Jeff and in how I survived his death. As her own maternal instincts increased and she imagined herself with an actual child in her arms, she couldn't fathom enduring such a loss. As she spent more and more time with me, she grew curious about the little boy I had lost, what he looked like, what his personality was like, what cute things he did, what I thought he would be like as an adult. She was very sensitive to my feelings in talking about a tender subject, and I was touched that she was so intrigued with him. I willingly shared my memories with her. There was really no one else in my life who would talk about him with me, so these conversations were special times. Together we went through an entire grocery bag and album full of pictures, while I explained the occasions and related any stories that came to mind. She even asked me several times if I would take her to the cemetery. But up until recently, as I have explained, I wasn't ready to do that.

Amy asked me to be her Lamaze coach, so we prepared for the arrival of the first grandchild together. Her dad and I were married a month before the baby was born, and, since she lived with us, we were "on duty" waiting for the onset of contractions. Her baby boy was born at 11:00 a.m. on July 11, 1991, and Amy named him Jeffrey. It was a gift to me to fill a void in my heart—to restore a

Jeffrey to my life—and a beautiful expression of understanding, honor, and love. Although different in temperament and personality, this Jeffrey amazingly has some physical similarities to his "Uncle" Jeffrey, and this Jeffrey is most precious to his Papa and me.

What is my life like today? God has restored abundantly, keeping His promise that He would fulfill every area of my life. At this writing, Jeffrey is five years old and has a little sister named Adora. This past Memorial Day I decided to take flowers to my son's grave, the first time in 26 years. Dennis went with me, along with Amy and the two children, Amy explaining to Jeffrey what a cemetery is, why we were going, and who was there—the little boy for whom he was named. After we had cleaned off the headstone and placed the flowers, Jeffrey looked at the name engraved there and said, "Look, that's just like my name!" I shed some tears and Jeff was concerned about that, asking why I was crying. Amy explained it was because I missed my boy. I told him he was the only Jeffrey I had now, so that made him even more special to me. He said, "It's OK, Grandma, you can take care of me sometimes!" Right before we left, after we had sat quietly for a moment, he said, "Shouldn't we say something to him? Should we pray?" That precious understanding and love meant everything to me.

After taking a few detours, Amy has given herself 100 percent to God, and it has changed her life. A big part of the change has come with her ability to forgive past offenses, as well as the offenders. One major reconciliation occurred recently between her and Paul, who is Jeff's father. Many hurtful words and actions which occurred after Amy became pregnant led to five years of hatred and distance. Once again they have become friends and Jeff has had the opportunity to know his dad. Amy has become very involved in church as a leader in our Youth Ministry and a choir member. It has been a wonderful transformation for her and a very great blessing to us as her parents, to finally see her happy and working toward the potential that God built into her.

Shana's growth and healing has also been an awesome thing to behold. Dennis has been instrumental in her ability to trust men again, as he has been a trustworthy father to her. She has emerged like a butterfly from its cocoon: in choir, on the worship team, a leader in the College and Young Adults Ministry, a missionary trip to the Philippines last year. She is now married to a great young man named Randall Carter, who has become another son to us.

Rob graduated from college in December of 1995 with a Business Administration degree and is now working for a roofing contractor. He is married to Carol, who has become like a daughter to us. They attend our church as well.

In October, 1993, my Dennis got saved—the first time he went to church with me. And he knew that God had gotten hold of him as he walked out of church that day a new man! Starting from ground zero, it is amazing how quickly he's grown. Our marriage was good before, but now it's complete—we are a team. It's been like finding the missing piece of a puzzle for me. We are learning and ministering together and through a prophetic word have been designated as "pillars" in our church. When God told me that he was giving Dennis to me as a gift, his salvation was the ribbon on the package.

In September, 1995, Dennis and I were candidates for presbytery, an honor for us. Out of the word we were given, God revealed how He had gifted me to "know" things. It explained so much about how I have been all my life.

> *Sharon, there are giftings inside of you that*
> *are prophetic and discerning. There's an*
> *ability inside you to know the mind and the*
> *will of God in the area of dreams and visions*
> *and hearing God's voice with your inner ear,*
> *in your spirit man. And there's been confusion*
> *because you haven't known how much of that*
> *has been God and how much of that has been*

your own imagination. You've had the gift to be able to look at somebody and be able to tell, almost at a moment's glance, if they were really true blue or if they were hypocritical or if they were turning in their hypocrisy. And it's caused you great concern. You've said, "God, I don't want to be critical." And God says, "Daughter, I'm tempering that gift, I'm giving you confidence in it, and you're going to know the mind and the will of God. You're going to know how to perceive My thoughts, perceive My ways, for I am making you one that sees in the Spirit. Now, don't fear any longer, but know I am speaking to you. You're going to see with your eyes and hear with your ears, and know in your spirit what I am saying. Be confident and bold. "

Rev. Scott Webster

God said He would fulfill *every* area of my life, which included my job. In May, 1992, I landed a job as an executive secretary for a director of a prestigious, worldwide marketing consulting company. It was a position to aspire to, in a company that provided beautiful surroundings, great benefits, the best salary I had ever earned, interesting and intelligent coworkers, and an insight into the workings of major corporations around the world. But there was a major problem—I got bored. Even in the times I was extremely busy (I like to be busy), I felt increasingly unfulfilled and frustrated. I felt that I was performing the same tasks that I had been doing for years, and for what? I felt useless, that I was wasting my time. More and more I wanted to be doing something for God. Rather than criticizing me or encouraging me to be satisfied, Dennis watched my restlessness and listened to my longing for something more. And he began to pray for me, that God would open up a door for me to be doing something that would, indeed, satisfy the desires of my heart. We both began to sense that God was stirring me up as a prelude to moving me.

My first opportunity came as our pastor asked me to produce a ministries manual for our network of churches. Although we had some prepared material for me to work with, it was necessary to start almost from scratch to produce the desired result. It was a huge challenge for me, but it was a labor of love. He offered to pay me, but my payment came in the satisfaction I felt as I saw the final product emerging. It was in the course of those months that our pastor got to know me better, and he eventually asked me to be his assistant. That's right, the same tasks that I had been doing, at about half the salary. But this time I knew it was where God wanted me. I am truly in my element, knowing that there is purpose and fulfillment in my work.

In April of 1996 at our women's retreat, I was called out on the very last morning. As you have now read about some of the events in my life during the '80s, you will see what a powerful word this is.

O, faithful servant, how long it took to get you to this place where you could open up and trust again. For the Lord says '84, '87, '89, and '90 were not good years for you. And you were damaged and scarred greatly in those times of the '80s and it caused you to draw in and it caused you to pull back and you didn't know what to do. But God says, "My Daughter, I Am greater. I Am greater than the '80s. I Am greater than '84, '87, and '89, and I have yet to begin a new thing on the inside of you, and you are going to find that out of your misery is going to come your ministry. For I Am preparing you and I Am grooming you and I Am getting you

*ready for something that is so mighty that
you yourself won't be able to believe what I
Am doing in you. But this day I Am releasing
you from the pain of the '80s. I Am releasing
you from the '80s so you can live in the '90s
and into 2000. . . because this thing has held
you long enough."*

Ruckins McKinley

The significance of these words had a dramatic effect as the depth of their meaning impacted me. Again, here was specific knowledge revealed by God, letting me know that He knew the pain, the scarring, the withdrawing, the struggling and not knowing what to do, and the years that were the worst during that time. He said that out of my misery would come my ministry and showed me that this book is a ministry out of my misery. The writing of this book, as I have stated, has brought tremendous healing to me. Since all through the writing I felt strongly that I should not disclose our life in the '80s, I wondered what process I would have to go through to erase the scars of that period of my life. Do you see the mercy of God as He wiped out the wounds of an entire decade in a moment of time? Something actually happened inside me. Think of carrying around a full backpack for a number of years. You are so used to its bulk and weight that you don't really notice it unless it bumps into something or someone asks why you are carrying it or the extra weight slows you down at particularly difficult times. Then, all of a sudden someone takes it from you, saying that you are released from this responsibility, and you suddenly feel freer and lighter, finally realizing what a useless burden you had been carrying. That's how I felt as I left that retreat without the excess baggage—at last set free.

Psalm 30

*I will extol You, O Lord, for You have lifted me
up, and have not let my foes rejoice over me.
O Lord My God, I cried out to You, and You
have healed me. O Lord, You have brought my
soul up from the grave; You have kept me
alive, that I should not go down to the pit.*

*Sing praise to the Lord, you saints of His,
and give thanks at the remembrance of His
Name. For His anger is but for a moment, and
His favor is for life; weeping may endure for a
night, but joy comes in the morning.*

*Now in my prosperity I said, "I shall never
be moved." Lord, by Your favor You have
made my mountain stand strong; You hid
Your face, and I was troubled.*

*I cried out to You, O Lord; and to the Lord I
made supplication: "What profit is there in my
blood, when I go down to the pit?
Will the dust praise You?
Will it declare Your truth?
Hear, O Lord, and have mercy on me;
Lord, be my helper!"
You have turned for me my mourning into
dancing;
You have put off my sackcloth and clothed me
with gladness, to the end that my glory may
sing praise to You and not be silent.*

**O Lord my God, I will give thanks to You
forever.**

Endorsements

"When you get ready to read a book through in one sitting, *From Tragedy to Triumph* is the one you need to reach for. This incredible and deeply spiritual story totally absorbs you from the very first page. Once you have finished it, you will see suffering and pain in a more comforting and empowering light. New beginnings can and do happen in our lives. *From Tragedy to Triumph* is a gift that fills you with the courage to believe that as never before."

Dr. David Cannistraci
Co-Pastor
Evangel Christian Fellowship

"Inspirational! A true story about one brave woman with life experiences that we can all relate to. A must read that will help you and everyone in your family to better understand the mysteries of life and death."

Capt. Roy Froom
Santa Clara County Sheriff's Office

"Strong, vibrant characters are the essence of this enthralling true story. They cause you to laugh, to cry, and sometimes to do both simultaneously. Their heartaches are poignant and their good times a cause for real celebration."

Dr. Jane Early

"This book is a testimonial to God's grace and faithfulness. Sharon has a message in this very personal experience, to every one of God's children. You will find hope and a new beginning as you read this book and let God heal you."

Dr. Emanuele Cannistraci
Senior Pastor
Evangel Christian Fellowship

"Healing, hope, and inspiration are what you can expect from reading this book! Sharon Gregory's testimony is the example of God's grace and plan for our lives. After reading this book, you will realize that no matter where you are or have been in your life, you can overcome anything. *From Tragedy to Triumph* will inspire you to press on!"

Stephanie Barbero

"Experiencing a great loss will either thrust you into a deeper relationship with God or drive you into bitterness and a life void of Him. Sharon Gregory's honest and vivid account of her life's deep pain and disappointments—foremost the death of her toddler––finds you thanking God for your own blessings and gives you the hope that He will always turn your tragedies into triumphs. This gripping story will give you courage, lift your spirit, and cause you to want to share with others the miracles of Christ."

Debbie Hall